REFORMING
THE CHURCH

REFORMING THE CHURCH

A SYNODAL WAY OF PROCEEDING

Serena Noceti

Paulist Press
New York / Mahwah, NJ

Cover image by Daniel Reiner / Shutterstock.com
Cover design by Sharyn Banks
Book design by Lynn Else

Library of Congress Cataloging-in-Publication Data
Names: Noceti, Serena, author.
Title: Reforming the church : a synodal way of proceeding / Serena Noceti.
Description: New York/Mahwah, NJ : Paulist Press, [2023] | Includes bibliographical references. | Summary: "Reforming the Church outlines the implications of an integral reform in a Synodal Church"—Provided by publisher.
Identifiers: LCCN 2022057409 (print) | LCCN 2022057410 (ebook) | ISBN 9780809156597 (paperback) | ISBN 9780809188192 (ebook)
Subjects: LCSH: Councils and synods. | Catholic Church, Pope (2013- : Francis) | Church renewal. | Francis, Pope, 1936–
Classification: LCC BV710 .N53 2023 (print) | LCC BV710 (ebook) | DDC 262.001/7—dc23/eng/20230329
LC record available at https://lccn.loc.gov/2022057409
LC ebook record available at https://lccn.loc.gov/2022057410

ISBN 978-0-8091-5659-7 (paperback)
ISBN 978-0-8091-8819-2 (e-book)

Published by Paulist Press
997 Macarthur Boulevard
Mahwah, New Jersey 07430
www.paulistpress.com

Printed and bound in the
United States of America

CONTENTS

CONTENTS

INTRODUCTION

Pope Francis teaches,

> To walk together is *the constitutive way* of the Church; *the figure* that enables us to interpret reality with the eyes and heart of God; *the condition* for following the Lord Jesus and being servants of life in this wounded time. The breath and pace of the Synod show what we are, and the dynamism of communion that animates our decisions; only in this way can we truly renew our pastoral ministry and adapt it to the mission of the Church in today's world; only in this way can we address the complexity of this time, thankful for the journey accomplished thus far, and determined to continue it with *parrhesia*.

With these words, spoken by Pope Francis at the assembly of the Italian Bishops' Conference in 2017, the International Theological Commission concludes its document "Synodality in the Life and Mission of the Church" (no. 120). Ecclesial renewal, which is now increasingly necessary, can only be accomplished by recognizing synodality as a constitutive dimension of the church and as its *modus vivendi et operandi*, thus committing to a reform of every aspect of pastoral life according to synodal logic and dynamics.

In his book *Synodality: A New Way of Proceeding in the Church*,[1] Venezuelan theologian Rafael Luciani outlines the fundamental theological principles that underpin Pope Francis's option for synodality and illustrates the pastoral and theological reasons for embracing the overall "synodalization" of every ecclesial dynamic, process, and structure. Today, making an option for synodality one's own means thinking systemically about the renewal and life of the ecclesial body, in the local churches, without limiting oneself to certain sectors or individual activities that would only make a partial change. It is precisely through synodality that the church manifests and reconfigures itself as the people of God in a continuous and communitarian process of *ecclesiogenesis*—a perpetual state of conversion and reform.

This book is closely related to the work of Rafael Luciani[2] and aims to offer concrete indications and suggestions to promote such a synodal "reconfiguration" in the local church and in the parish. The first two chapters recall the fundamental dynamics of a synodal church, a church of encounter and listening that walks together (Greek *syn-*, with), thanks to the contribution of all the baptized (interaction), toward a common understanding of the faith (*consensus fidelium, sensus fidei*). Within this horizon, both the ways of renewing the self-awareness of those involved (ordained ministers and laypeople) and ecclesial relations (chapters 3 and 4) and the lines of reform of diocesan and parish structures (chapter 5) are then outlined in very concrete ways. The two registers of synodal conversion and structural reforms for effective synodality interact and interpenetrate for the realization of the missionary and synodal reform to which Pope Francis calls the church.

To be realized, the "option for synodality" needs the voice of the laypeople—of women, of young people, of those who dissent

Introduction

and contest, of the poor and marginalized, and of all those who for centuries have not been recognized for "doing church." This calls for a ministerial reform that implements and fulfills the vision of ordained ministry and the subjectuality of the laypeople outlined by the Second Vatican Council and that recognizes the development of lay ministries—especially of women—that have greatly enriched local churches throughout the world since the Council.

At the same time, a new "synodal figure" of the church must mature. According to Roland Barthes, in order to describe and understand a theme, it is useful to use the category of the "figure" starting from the Greek definition of a "model" or "pattern," that is, to focus attention on the "gesture of the body or figure—in this case a collective body—caught in movement."[3] This type of approach allows us to go beyond the simple static description of the subject in favor of an interpretation of the process and relationships that occur. It is a matter of thinking of an "ecclesial figure" that is "synodically trans/figured," thanks to the progressive maturing of a new collective consciousness of the "ecclesial We," and thanks to the courageous change of certain central structures of ecclesial life (parish, formation of the clergy, liturgy, pastoral councils, and so forth). There are ecclesial subjects—men and women—who interact and generate together to bring about a new "church figure" but, at the same time, a change of certain institutions that are still an expression of the Gregorian-Tridentine ecclesiological vision, and to support the renewal of the ecclesial mentality and experience. Synodal meetings or events—a sign of the "ecclesial body on the move"—become an expression and realization of a constitutive dimension of being a synodal church, moments in which one learns to be "church together," people of God on the move (chapter 6). The synodal church lives by a certainty: together we understand the gospel; together we co-construct the community by the power of the

Spirit; together we fulfill our mission of service to the kingdom of God; together we walk.

This book is intended to be a contribution to the reconfiguration of ecclesial relations and participatory structures, of decision-making and communication forms, so that they may be effectively synodal: an undertaking that goes far beyond the celebration of a synod and that requires awareness of the complexity of the task and a decisive assumption of responsibility, creativity, and courage. As the document of the International Theological Commission concludes,

> The *parrhesía* of the Spirit required the People of God on its synodal journey is the trust, frankness and courage to "enter into the expanse of God's horizon" in order to "ensure that a sacrament of unity exists in the world and that man is therefore not destined for dispersion and confusion." The lived and enduring experience of synodality is, for the People of God, a source of the joy promised by Jesus, a catalyst of new life, the springboard for a new phase of missionary commitment. (no. 121)

1

The Name of the Church Is "Synod"

A PROGRESSIVE REDISCOVERY

The main reason for the renewed interest[1] in the theme of synodality is the attention given to it by Pope Francis since the beginning of his pontificate.[2] The concept of synodality is not present in the documents of the Second Vatican Council, and most of the studies dedicated to this theme are quite recent. Only in the 1990s and the first years of the new millennium do we witness a progressive flowering of research, initially of a juridical and historical nature—an example is the volume *Synod and Synodality*, fruit of a conference held in Bruges in 2003—and subsequently in systematic theology.[3] These studies examined various experiences of ecclesial synodality, such as the periodic synods of bishops, instituted by Paul VI at the time of the Council;[4] the numerous diocesan synods convened for the reception of Vatican II in the local churches;[5] and the activities of pastoral councils, presbyteral councils, and pastoral consultations and assemblies, all of which are instruments of participation of the people of God recommended by the Council. At the same time, research has been enriched by comparisons with the synodal practices of both the Orthodox churches and the churches of the Reformation, along with the principles that guide those practices. Most Christian churches already function in synodal forms, making use of synodal institutions and processes, although in highly varied ways and with different presuppositions.[6]

Less frequent have been the studies with an ecclesiological perspective. These studies, by recovering the biblical foundations and examining the various forms of synodality in church history, have focused especially on the nature of the church, the subjects having a voice in ecclesial life, the development of synodal relations, the relationship with episcopal collegiality, and the pastoral challenges presented by the recovery of synodality as a "constitutive dimension of the church." We mention, among others, the studies produced by Hervé Legrand, Gilles Routhier, Jean Marie Tillard,[7] and the 2005 congress of the Italian Theological Association.[8] This first phase of the research involved only a few theologians, mainly European. These pioneers met subdued resistance from most other theologians and received no support from the magisterium, but we are now witnessing a proliferation of studies on a diversity of topics, using very different approaches regarding theological categories and pastoral implications.[9]

Pope Francis and Synodality

The references to synodality have increased steadily in the speeches of Pope Francis, and synodality has become increasingly evident in the strategic pastoral choices of his pontificate. The pope has first sought to renew the way the synods of bishops are conducted, starting with the Synod on the Family, which was celebrated in two stages. The renewal continued with the Synod on Young People, which is integral to the 2021–23 Synod, whose very theme is ecclesial synodality: *For a Synodal Church: Communion, Participation, Mission*. At the level of practice, the most important change is the strengthening of the phase of listening to the people of God, as evidenced by the two questionnaires of the Synod on the Family, the preassembly of the youth synod, the involvement of more than eighty thousand people in the local churches and the 270 preparatory meetings for the Amazon synod, and the broad involvement of all the faithful in dioceses throughout the world for the 2021–23 Synod. The working dynamic during the synodal assemblies has been reshaped into a spiritual experience, aimed at discerning the voice of the Spirit in the moments of listening and the work of the *circuli minores*. The pope has also urged the local churches to promote local synodal processes, which have been especially evident in Germany, Italy, Australia, and Latin America.

Some documents also contain clear statements showing the links between "church reform," "pastoral conversion," and "synodality" and illustrating the changes in mentality, practices, and structures that are needed to achieve a meaningful synodal experience capable of promoting the necessary ecclesial renewal.[10] In his "Address on the Occasion of the Anniversary of the Institution of the Synod of Bishops" (October 17, 2015), Pope Francis stated clearly, "The path of synodality is the path that God expects from the church of the third millennium."[11] An especially significant document is the apostolic constitution *Episcopalis Communio* (2018),[12] in which Pope Francis clearly distinguishes between "episcopal collegiality" and "ecclesial synodality." He situates the Synod of Bishops within the broader horizon of synodality as a form of church. Understood as a *modus vivendi et operandi* of the whole people of God, synodality requires other moments and institutions that allow for greater participation in the making of decisions. "The Synod of Bishops is the point of convergence of this dynamic of listening, which is conducted at all levels of the life of the church."[13] However, synodality is not reducible to synodal events involving a few bishops advising the pope, nor does it simply mean inviting a few lay representatives and ordained ministers to take part in diocesan synods that remain extraordinary events in the life of the local church. Rather, synodality must permeate all contexts of "becoming church," from local churches to the universal church. Synodality demands rethinking and revitalizing all the participatory and representative structures of the various components of the people of God; and it must do so in all the different contexts in which the church expresses its life, conducts its research, and coordinates its actions, from pastoral councils to episcopal conferences.

The Reception of Vatican II

The document of the International Theological Commission, "Synodality in the Life and Mission of the Church," published in 2018, offers the most articulate and complete framework for understanding synodality.[14] It provides the theological presuppositions flowing from Scripture and ecclesial Tradition; it clarifies the pertinent terms and concepts and distinguishes synodality from collegiality, participation, communion, and coresponsibility; it treats the ways in which synodality should be implemented and describes the spirituality that should characterize all ecclesial subjects involved in synodal events and processes. Constantly referring to the Second Vatican Council, the document "puts forward the theological foundations of synodality in conformity with the ecclesiological doctrine of Vatican II, linking them with the perspective of the pilgrim and missionary People of God and with the mystery of Church as communion, in relation to the Church's distinctive characteristics: unity, holiness, Catholicity and apostolicity. Lastly it goes into the link between the participation of all the members of the People of God in the mission of the Church and the exercise of authority by their Pastors" (no. 10). Systematic theology's reflections on the synodal church and on the changes to be made in the *forma ecclesiae* and pastoral practices so that synodality characterizes the church at all levels constitute a key element for the reception of Vatican II and for the hermeneutics of the conciliar documents.

It is true that the term *synodality* is absent from the corpus of the texts of Vatican II; the documents speak only of the "Synod of Bishops" (CD 5) and "episcopal collegiality" (LG 22, CD 36). Nevertheless, working for and as a "synodal church" allows us to bring to fulfillment the ecclesiological vision of *Lumen Gentium*, some principles of which have been "suspended" or "contravened" in the last few decades (for example, the relationship between collegiality and primacy, the agency of local churches as subjects, and the church as "people of God" as the guiding vision of the Council's ecclesiology). With the drafting of *Christus Dominus* 5 by the Council, after the publication of *Apostolica Sollicitudo* by Paul VI on September 15, 1965, the Synod of Bishops came to be understood as an instrument at the service of the Petrine primacy and not as an expression of episcopal collegiality, as some Council Fathers had hoped. These developments contributed to divorcing the activity of the Synod of Bishops from the usual dynamics of the life of the local churches.[15] The construction site of the reception of Vatican II is still open: the ecclesiological vision proposed in chapter II of the Constitution on the Church has not yet been fully accepted either in its main lines—the self-understanding of the church as the people of God, the relationship between pastors and the faithful, and so forth—or in its pastoral implications.

The reform desired by the Council is still incomplete. Synodality allows and seeks the active participation of all the *christifideles*, as indicated by *Lumen Gentium* 12, and it encourages the development of an ecclesiology *from* the local churches. Synodality inspires cooperation between laity and ordained ministers in carrying out the ecclesial mission, and it calls for overcoming the hierarchical, pyramidal vision that marked the second millennium of the church's history. Since the 1990s, the hermeneutics of the pontifical magisterium has undoubtedly stressed a universalist perspective, adopting a christological interpretation of the ministry and action of bishops and priests vis-à-vis the people of God. It has shown a preference for the more generic notion of *communio*, to the detriment of the category "people of God" chosen by Vatican II, as well as to the detriment of the theology of the local church.

The option for synodality expressed by Pope Francis is helping to define a new phase in the reception of Vatican II and in the implementation of its demands for reform.

A SYNODAL FORM OF CHURCH

"There can be no life of the church, no expression of ecclesial being, except as a synodal event."[16] These words declaring synodality to be an essential element of the church's nature raise important questions: What are the reasons for affirming that synodality is an inherent dimension of ecclesial life or that the synodal form is a basic form of church? Why has this central feature of ecclesial existence been forgotten for centuries? To answer these questions, we need ecclesiological reflection that involves systematic theology but is open to the contributions of sociology and the philosophy of language.[17]

"Synodality" is an abstract concept with various meanings: "the idea of synodality has been widely studied and has been defined in a thousand ways" (S. Dianich). It is sometimes considered to be "a property of the church that derives from its communal nature" (A. Borras); at other times it is related directly to "collegiality," even though the subjects of synodality (the whole people of God) are different from the subjects of collegiality (the bishops). "Synodality" must also be distinguished from other concepts such as *communion, participation, co-responsibility, sharing,* and *listening.* These are all aspects of the dynamic that characterizes the synodal form of church, but they cannot be identified with synodality. Etymologically, the Greek word *syn/odos* signifies a "journey made together" or, more literally, a "shared path." It thus refers to the dynamic relationship that exists among several subjects who are working together to reach a destination. Synodality has always been present in the church's history, and this "walking together" has taken various concrete forms. In the course of time, different subjects have been seen as primarily responsible for exercising the dynamic by which the church tackles difficult problems, corrects erroneous teachings, and heals intra-ecclesial divisions. How should we understand "synodality" now in the twenty-first century, in the light of Vatican II and its ecclesiology?[18]

A Constitutive Dimension and a Unique Dynamic

It may be useful first to consider the adjective *synodal* rather than the abstract noun *synodality* as we bear in mind the Council's ecclesiological affirmations regarding the constitutive principle (proclamation), the subjects, and the dynamics of development. These themes are treated not only in *Lumen Gentium* but also in *Ad Gentes, Dei Verbum, Sacrosanctum Concilium,* and *Gaudium et*

Spes (chapter IV). When we speak of "synodal form," we are referring to an "essential dimension" of church, as the document of the International Theological Commission makes clear: it concerns the very nature and dynamic of the relationships that constitute the church. It is therefore not enough to refer simply to "communion" because in the synodal form of church, the very processes of institutionalization are at stake. Synodality entails the "historical making" of the "ecclesial 'We,'" a collective subject that comes alive in the communicational dynamics of faith and through a distinctive interaction between the empirical level of ecclesial life and the mystical, eschatological level. The church has a communal essence and exists in synodal forms; synodality is the church's *modus vivendi et operandi.* These various aspects, which are distinguishable but not separable, are kept closely interconnected by the communicational dynamics of faith. Communion functions at the level of the essential interior dynamic characterizing relations with God, between persons, and between local churches. Synodality has to do with the empirically observable processes of communication, discernment, decision-making, and collective implementation. Ecclesial communion is born from the acceptance of the announcement of salvation (see Acts 2; 1 John 1:1–4; LG 17), and it thrives by the ongoing dynamic of communication of faith and in faith among believers, ranging from catechesis to eucharistic liturgy and from pastoral assemblies to serving the needs of others. Synodality is not simply an expression of "church communion"; it is the specific form and dynamic of the life and action of the ecclesial body, a communion that derives from a communicational dynamic and that prospers by the mutual communication among all Christians. The two texts of Vatican II in which this dynamic of "becoming church" is expounded are *Lumen Gentium* 12, on the prophetic *munus* of the people of God, and *Dei Verbum* 8, on the subjects involved in the development of the *Traditio Ecclesiae*. These texts conceive the church as constructed jointly by all the *christifideles*, with their different charisms and ministries: all the faithful are subjects of the word, starting from the obedience of faith to the gospel received.[19]

The Intersection of the Forms and the Processes of "Making Church"

To understand the dimensions and forms of synodality, we do well to take note of a statement of John Chrysostom that is often only partially quoted. The complete expression reads, *"ekklesía gar systèmatos kai synódou estìn ónoma,"* "church means both assembling together and walking together."[20] The first term (*systèmatos*) has to do with meeting together, agreeing, and sharing, while the second (*synódou*) has to do with walking together. In the synodal form of church, we must simultaneously consider both levels with their distinct dynamics and forms. The church's name—that is, its recognized and proclaimed identity—is given in a sort of hendiadys, a twinning of two correlated aspects, both constructed with the Greek prefix *syn-*, signifying relationship. The first word (*systèmatos*) stresses "standing together" and the other (*synódou*) "shared dynamism."

    a.   The *first level* of synodality, therefore, is that of *understanding/grasping the faith together*. All baptized persons participate in the prophetic *munus* of Christ; anointed by the Spirit, they become subjects co-constituting the church because they contribute to the understanding and proclamation of the gospel according to their specific charisms and ministries (see LG 12). The *sensus fidei ecclesiae* (that is, the sense of the collective subject, the ecclesial "We") is rooted in the *sensus fidei fidelium*, which involves an ongoing dynamic that yields an ever more developed and differentiated understanding down through the generations and across different cultures. The church is continually oriented toward the search for the *consensus fidelium*,[21] which emerges on the empirical level from the attestations of faith of all believers; the believers are in turn fortified and guided by those in the church who have received from the Spirit a certain charisma of truth, the bishops (see DV 8). The synodal church is experienced and organized in "hermeneutical communities" that allow all members—ordained ministers and laypeople—to participate effectively in understanding the faith, according to their diverse charisms and ministries. In this way, a reciprocal dynamic unfolds between the *sensus fidei* and the magisterium (DV 10),[22] but for this to happen, we must start from baptism in defining subjectivity in the church, and not from the sacrament of orders. The reason is that every one of the faithful is an "actor" in understanding and announcing the faith; every one of the faithful is a co-constituting subject of the ecclesial "We," which is always plural and interconnected. Nevertheless, the service of ordained ministers is necessary to preserve the apostolic roots of ecclesial identity and to safeguard the unity of the "We" in the service of the "one."

b. The *second level* at which ecclesial synodality is realized is that of *walking together and working together*. The Second Vatican Council thoroughly rethought the theology of the ordained ministry in the people of God, including its nature and the forms of its exercise. The Council recovered the subjectivity of the laity after centuries of marginalization and lack of recognition. It recognized both laity and ministers as having equal dignity (see LG 32), and it outlined the forms of fruitful cooperation (see LG 37). Most importantly, it defined the horizon of the shared mission that can be accomplished only if laity and ordained are united as coresponsible agents. As LG 30 aptly expresses, "*ut cuncti suo modo ad commune opus unanimiter cooperentur*" ("that all cooperate together in their own way for the common good"). The *synodal* church is a church of *synergy*: those who walk together cooperate according to the specific character of their ecclesial subjectivity. Synodality overcomes the pyramidal, hierarchical vision of church that separated *ecclesia docens* and *ecclesia discens*, leaving only active subjects (the clergy) who taught and subordinate subjects (the laity) who were expected to follow their lead obediently. The twofold level of reflection and action that characterizes the synodal church requires a rethinking of decision-making processes so that they are in accord with the ancient Justinian legislative principle, accepted by the early church, "*quod omnes tangit, ab omnibus tractari [et approbari] debet*"[23] ("What affects all must be treated and approved by all").

The Synodal Church, a "Church of the Con-"

The synodal church is a "church of the *con-*" (corresponding to the Greek prefix *syn-*): it grows in the *sensus fidei* according to what Newman happily defined with the Latin word *con/spiratio*, and it operates thanks to the "*syn/ergy*" (from the Greek *syn/energeia*) between ordained ministers and lay men and women of different charisms, cultures, and states of life. The word of each and everyone in the church is necessary for the gospel to be understood and proclaimed in a new way; the service rendered by each and every one is essential for the construction of a body that is coordinated and connected in ministry, formation, and liturgical life. However, all members of the body attest to the faith and contribute to the ecclesial mission according to the ministerial specificity proper to them. The document of the International Theological Commission describes this dynamism in terms of the interaction between "all" (the faithful), "some" (theologians, pastoral workers, counselors in various participatory bodies), and "one" (bishop, presbyter).[24] Neither the *munus docendi* nor the *munus regendi* of the ordained ministers ("one") can be isolated from the word of faith, the service of the people of God, or an inclusive synergistic dynamic (see LG 25, 27): these are all at the service of and operate in correlation with the prophetic and royal *munera* of the people of God and of all the subjects who co-constitute it (see LG 12). The synodality of the church unfolds in the synergy between the magisterial, pastoral function of the bishops and the royal, prophetic function of the whole people of God, a people who journey in faith, understand the gospel in light of the signs of the times, and fulfill their messianic mission in history.

Among the believers who co-constitute the synodal church in faith, the dynamics of the communication of faith are multidirectional and asymmetrical. Each baptized person is a subject who listens to the Word of God and to the words of other subjects of the ecclesial "We." Each subject is a speaker in this communications network, the bearer of a unique and necessary word. Ordained ministers render a particular service for the institutionalized ecclesial "We" by guaranteeing the apostolic and catholic identity of the ecclesial body. Given the "co-essentiality of hierarchical and charismatic gifts,"[25] however, this asymmetry present in the church's communicational network must never result in a system of exclusion or sacralized hierarchicalism.

Establishing the synodal form of church within the framework of the ecclesiology of Vatican II requires overcoming the unidirectional model of communication that has characterized the many centuries of the Gregorian-Tridentine understanding of church. The fields for the exercise of authority and power should be defined in the Christian community only by correlation of the three vectors: "one-with-all," "some-one," and "some-all." The "one all" relationship and the corresponding obedience and adhesion attested to in the "all one" relationship encapsulate their basic relations to the saying-proclaiming of the faith, but these need to be placed within this more complex framework of ecclesial, communicative, and participative relations in the exercise of an authentic co-responsibility, for only these are "ordered and responsible relations."[26]

CONDITIONS FOR AUTHENTIC SYNODALITY

The sociocultural and ecclesial context provides motivation and momentum toward reform, which requires both a change of mentality (pastoral conversion) and a renewal of practices and structures in a synodal perspective and spirit. Reform and synodality appear as inseparable in the ecclesiological-pastoral vision of Pope Francis.

The Synodal Reform Necessary for Today's Church

The rethinking of the church in synodal form is prompted primarily by changes in society and the church.

First, we live at a time when social structures and the sense of citizenship are shaped by a widespread democratic mindset that stresses participation and equality, even as many Western democracies are suffering a crisis of representation. The organizational models in the Catholic Church, in contrast, still mostly resemble those of the monarchies of earlier centuries: they consist of closed systems with statically defined roles, in which the asymmetry of functions is understood as a rigid hierarchy. We live in an age when the logic of traditional "kyriocentric" and patriarchal authority is rightly contested and resisted, in full recognition of women's subjectivity, whereas in the church the space for women to speak and decide is limited and inadequate. A synodal church makes it possible for everyone to participate effectively in the complex deliberative processes and to be involved in hermeneutic communities.

Second, we are living in an era in which religions are regaining public space, presence, and voice. The religious dimension of existence is recognized as significant for personal and social development but often is considered only as a matter of personal adherence. "Postsecular society," "second secularization," and "late secularization" are three expressions that describe this cultural season. Nevertheless, it is a time when people's experience of the divine, their expression of faith, and their relation to the church are finding different modalities. Individuals want to move forward in freedom and autonomy, going beyond static forms and categorical formulations of doctrine.[27] They want a synodal church that guarantees space for mutual recognition, for posing existential questions, and for listening to the manifold answers of faith. They want a synodal church that supports gradual and partial belonging rather than standardization that disillusions many individuals of late modernity who are suspicious of institutions that claim to be all-inclusive. They want a church in which members can speak openly and frankly, a church that is open to a search for meaning and that actively involves them.

Third, the Catholic Church has now, sixty years after the start of Vatican II, become a "world church," as Karl Rahner predicted after the Council. It is no longer a Western church diffused everywhere, but rather a church incarnated in the different cultures of the world. The inherited colonial forms must be eradicated so that the *communio ecclesiarum* is authentic and so that a lively exchange exists between the different ways of being Christian. A synodal church can enhance the specific contributions of the different local churches; it can promote the inculturation of the faith and church ministry; and it can develop differentiated organizational methods that respect the customs and sensibilities of diverse peoples. The recognition of pluralism in the ecclesial tradition can be a significant maturing process for the Catholic Church.

The final reason for synodal reform is the dramatic revelation of sexual, financial, and conscience abuse that we as Catholics have seen over the last two decades.[28] By examining what has happened, we can understand more clearly how it was possible to inflict such deep wounds on the ecclesial body, and we will comprehend the resistance to synodal conversion that still exists today. The abuse in the church has shown the radical limitation of an "ecclesial system" rooted in top-down power dynamics. In its management of authority, the system is structured according to a sacralized, hierarchical-monarchical logic that lacks transparency and accountability. It is the opposite of a synodal church. In this pyramidal system of ecclesial relations, those who have power are accountable only to those who occupy higher positions in the hierarchical structure, and there is no sharing of information. A "culture of secrecy" has covered up huge scandals and defended the interests of a few to the detriment of the victims. This system depends not only on individuals, but on a noncooperative, top-down ecclesial system in which a few men—the clergy—enjoy unquestioned discretionary authority. In many respects, the organization of the church continues to be the same as it was after the Council of Trent, since in many places the main structures of church life—parish, seminary, priestly celibacy—have not been rethought and renewed in accord with Vatican II.[29]

Synodal Conversion of All *Christifideles* and Reform of Structures

"Synodality is not just a group of people walking together toward a common goal; it is a community trying to find its way together through collective discernment."[30] For this to happen, certain preconditions are necessary regarding both people and structures.

First, the *laity*, as authentic "*synodoi*," must be recognized as fully fledged subjects in and for a synodal church. Their contribution—in charisms, professional skills, and life experiences—is unique and irreplaceable, and their participation is "indispensable," as the International Theological Commission states clearly.[31] In particular, the issue of gender must be addressed: since Vatican II, the subjectivity of public, competent, and authoritative speech of women has finally been recognized but is still not always adequately valued. There will be no synodal church or church reform without women's contribution and without acknowledgment of the patriarchal heritage and the androcentric forms of exclusion that still afflict the Catholic Church and deprive ordinary pastoral life of women's valuable contributions.

Second, the role of the bishop (and priests) in the promotion of a synodal church must be rethought. As the guarantor of the *consensus fidelium*, the bishop must preside over the ecclesial process, discern what emerges, safeguard the apostolicity of the faith, and pronounce the word of the ecclesial "We." However, bishops do not always appear to be sufficiently trained in the transformative and cooperative type of leadership that needs to be exercised in an institution as complex and multiform as a local church. The conscience of some (laypeople) and of others (ordained ministers, primarily bishops) must be properly formed; it must develop a sense of belonging and co-responsibility (empowerment) even as it increases mutual recognition of the subjectivity of all in rights and duties (entitlement).[32]

Third, a truly effective synodality will develop only when "synodal consciousness" is translated into *"synodal forms"* of participation. This requires passing from the laity's baptismal "being part" of the church to their active "taking part" in the life of the church, which means "co-participating" in listening, discernment, and consensus through appropriate *"synodal structures and institutions."* To this end, intermediate bodies (pastoral councils, presbyteral councils, episcopal conferences) and dynamic assemblies in parishes and dioceses should be strengthened, as should the contexts of lay representation in which public opinion can mature.

Finally, the *decision-making processes* must be reorganized organically so that they allow for the contributions and the interactions of the one, the some, and the all at various stages of the process, which are the following: (1) defining/clarifying the objective (involving all, some, and one); (2) gathering relevant information regarding choices (all, some experts, and members of pastoral councils); (3) outlining the feasible options (some); (4) defining the criteria for judgment (one with the help of some theologians); and (5) evaluating the options proposed, so that in the end one can make a decision (decision-taking).[33]

The implementation of structural reforms is essential to achieve a synodal church. The issue of the consultative vote of the laity[34] must therefore be examined in depth, and the issue of power, the most taboo subject of church life today, must be addressed. "Power is the most important aspect of a society's structure"[35] because all social systems are defined by the acquisition of authority roles, the distribution and hierarchicalization of power(s), and the foundation and justification of power and related roles. The church has for centuries institutionalized a pyramidal form of authority in which the "one," with the instrumental mediation of "some," rules over "all." As we have seen, synodality means keeping all possible directions copresent and co-related in the processes of communication in faith, without misconstruing functions or unjustifiably leveling specific ministries. However, talk about synodality implies being aware of one's own relation to others and to the other (in the ministers, in the one, in the some): by this awareness the faithful experience the collective identity of the people of God, a community of believers.

In an interview with *Il Regno*, Carlos Schickendantz, an Argentine theologian now teaching in Santiago de Chile, stated that the credibility of the church today depends not only on how it is structured[36] (given that it must be an exemplary sign of the logic of the kingdom of God), but also on how it implements its procedures, treats people, and manages power. All these activities make it urgently necessary to express, implement, and develop a synodal form of church.

2

From *Consensus Ecclesiae* to the "We" of Christian Faith

In the apostolic exhortation *Evangelii Gaudium*, the programmatic document of his pontificate, Pope Francis clearly affirms that all the baptized are full ecclesial subjects and so are co-responsible in the dynamics of understanding the gospel and evangelizing today's world. All *christifideles* are actively involved in the messianic mission of Jesus, and they become participants in the *tria munera* of Christ through the sacraments of Christian initiation. As a "messianic people" (LG 9) with priestly, prophetic, and royal roles, the church fulfills the same mission as Jesus of Nazareth. Those who profess their faith in Jesus take on his "cause," the realization of the kingdom of God in human history. They cooperate with other baptized persons so that the church becomes a sign and an instrument of God's kingdom, its seed and beginning. Pope Francis affirms that all the baptized, the entire people of God, are subjects of the church's word-and-action, and he grounds this affirmation on the perspective in the opening of the second chapter of *Lumen Gentium*. In *Evangelii Gaudium* he refers twice—with explicit quotations in 119 and 130—to LG 12, which treats of the prophetic *munus* and the *sensus fidei*.[1]

This passage is central for the ecclesiological vision of Vatican II, but it was marginalized in magisterial documents during the pontificates of Paul VI, John Paul II, and Benedict XVI.[2] This declaration of principles is fundamental, but it has met with only limited reception on the level of the practice and self-definition of the whole church. There has been significant postconciliar theological debate on the subject,[3] with obvious differences in approach and sensitivity, but the debate has mostly supported the theses of the International Theological Commission's document on synodality.[4] Sixty years after the start of the Council, the question of the *sensus fidei/fidelium* appears absolutely central to the conception of a synodal church, even if further theological reflection is needed, as well as practical implementation that can enlighten theoretical understanding.[5] Once *Lumen Gentium* 12 is genuinely and widely received,[6] the understanding of the dynamics of synodality will mature; conversely, the promotion of synodal conversion and the creation of synodal structures will make it clear that *Lumen Gentium* is capable of illuminating and motivating the collective effort of all. Vatican II was a "council *of* the church *on* the church"; it recognizes all the people of God as full subjects of ecclesial life and its reform. Thus, its reception gives dynamism to the synodal church, linking it closely to the *sensus fidelium*, which is also expressed and manifested in this way.[7]

LUMEN GENTIUM 12

When the Council Fathers speak of the *sensus fidei/fidelium* in *Lumen Gentium* 12, they are referring to a theme that is not entirely new. Melchior Cano, in presenting the *"ecclesia catholica"* among the *loci theologici*, referred to the *"fidelium communis sensus"* and the *"sensus omnium fidelium,"* and subsequently so did Robert Bellarmine and several enlightened Catholic theologians of the nineteenth and twentieth centuries.[8] Recourse to the *sensus ecclesiae* and the *fidelium conspiratio* was central to the promulgation of the two Marian dogmas.[9] However, the Council Fathers' approach to the subject was unprecedented: both the location of the reflection (within discourse about the people of God) and the development of the argument (indicating the subjects and dynamics of ecclesial life)[10] departed from the traditional post-Tridentine and legalistic views.

The entire church participates in the prophetic *munus* of Christ. The church is the communion of believers who hear the Word of God that convokes one and all. Through the gift of the Spirit and by virtue of a specific and singular charism, every baptized person participates in the prophetic *munus* and so is actively involved[11] in the task of proclaiming the gospel and interpreting the salvific meaning of revelation.

All the *christifideles*—both ordained ministers and laypeople —participate in a collective dynamic through a twofold communion that matures in the communication of faith in which all are co-participants; they interact in a tending toward com/union that is achieved thanks to the contribution of every believing subject who co-constitutes the church:

> The entire body of the faithful, anointed as they are
> by the Holy One (cf. 1 John 2:20, 27), cannot err in

matters of belief. They manifest this special property by means of the supernatural discernment of the faith of all the people when, "from the Bishops down to the last of the lay faithful," they show universal agreement in matters of faith and morals. That discernment in matters of faith is aroused and sustained by the Spirit of truth. It is exercised under the guidance of the sacred teaching authority, in faithful and respectful obedience to which the people of God accepts that which is not just the word of men but truly the word of God (cf. 1 Thess 2:13). Through it, the people of God adheres unwaveringly to the faith given once and for all to the saints (cf. Jude 3), penetrates it more deeply with right thinking, and applies it more fully in its life.

The faith is "common" because it is accepted and personally appropriated by each of the ecclesial components and because it is made real and possible for the collective subject by the copresence of all the ecclesial subjects. This text adopts a deliberately pneumatological approach: the Holy Spirit is at once the source of the various gifts for the common good and the promoter and guarantor of communion with God and among persons, a communion that is always *in fieri*, always maturing and growing.

The Holy Spirit sanctifies and leads the people of God and enriches it with virtues, but, "allotting his gifts to everyone according as He wills" (1 Cor 12:11), He distributes special graces among the faithful of every rank. By these gifts He makes them fit and ready to undertake the various tasks and offices which contribute to the renewal and building up of the Church, according to the words of the Apostle: "The manifestation of the

Spirit is given to everyone for the profit of all" (1 Cor 12:7).

This conception helps us to understand how the synodal church works by means of the *sensus fidei* in the *perichoresis* of individual persons/subjects and the collective subject (the ecclesial "We"), and how authentic reform develops precisely through the synodal dynamics of communication and participation.

LISTENING TO THE WORD OF GOD THROUGH THE WORDS OF OTHER BELIEVERS

The church is the people of God, and it is born of the dynamic of evangelization carried out by all the baptized: every Christian has received and welcomed the gospel proclamation and so has become a participant in the prophetic *munus* of Christ. Every Christian is therefore responsible for keeping the gospel word alive down through the generations (see 1 John 1:1–4; Luke 1:1–4; 1 Cor 15:1–4). After the first generation, one becomes a Christian by means of a *paradosis*, a "handing over" of the faith that is never the mere repetition of abstract content, an inert deposit of timeless truths, or a complete set of doctrines and moral notions. Rather, the *paradosis* happens through the testimony of believers who belong to the ecclesial body that is the true and proper custodian of the apostolic faith. Ecclesial life is preserved by transmitting the apostolic faith in Christ and inviting others to participate in his body. The church thrives by continually receiving and transmitting the living Word (see DV 1; LG 17) to those who are not believers, and by always seeking a greater and richer understanding (see LG 12; DV 8) of the gospel that has been announced, believed, and celebrated thanks to the dynamic communication of faith and in faith among believers as they are confronted with new languages and new challenges that come from history and the world's cultures.[12] At the heart of the *sensus fidei* is the twofold process of communication and "identification" that makes it possible for the church—in the course of generations—to understand itself as a historical reality that is in the process of becoming and, at the same time, to exercise its specific mission in the world.[13] *Lumen Gentium* 12 helps us to see the three dynamics that are at work: *sensus fidei ecclesiae, sensus fidei fidelium,* and *sensus fidei fidelis.* The three are related but should be distinguished in understanding the process:

The *sensus fidei ecclesiae* (understanding "church" as an institutionalized, collective historical subject) has a logical and chronological priority: the church is rooted in and characterized by the Christian faith that is common to all, and it is marked by the *sensus fidei*, which consists of a collective consciousness, that is, a "symbolic universe" that is the matrix of all socially objective and subjectively valid meanings.[14] The faith of the Christian is always personal ("I believe"), but at the same time it is ecclesial in content and form ("This is our faith; this is the faith of the church. We glory in professing it."), and it is rooted in the apostolic faith. All Christians are such because of the faith they received through the church: their identity as believers is given in the church and as church, but their specific identities are delineated and determined according to their personal appropriation and reexpression, that is, according to their personal traits (circumstances, age, culture, gender, level of conscience formation, and so forth) and their specific charisms, so that all believers can contribute to the ecclesial "We" according to their specific gifts. The *sensus fidelium* is thus found at the crossroads between each believer's story of faith and belonging, on the one hand, and the development of the content of the *Traditio Ecclesiae*, on the other, as this takes place in the *perichoresis* between the individual believing subjects who co constitute the church and the "ecclesial We" that is the bearer and proper subject of the *memoria Iesou*.

THE "WE" OF CHRISTIAN FAITH

The challenge now is to live in the form of a synodal, participatory, inclusive church in which believers are capable of permanent learning from each other. As Romano Guardini wrote,

> There is no such thing as an isolated, independent faith. Our personal faith feeds its life into the life of the totality of faith that surrounds us and flows from the present back to the past. The church is the "We in faith"; it is the community of believers. Not only Christian prayer, but Christian faith must also say "We," for it too is rooted in the "We" taken as totality. The We is more than the sum of the individuals; it is the movement produced by the individuals. One hundred persons who present themselves to God as *ekklesia* represent more than the addition of a hundred individuals; they form a living community, a believing community.[15]

The *sensus fidelium* (that is, the faith of all believers) and the *sensus fidei ecclesiae* require the contribution of all the baptized: all believers share their understanding of faith (*sensus fidei fidelis*). All are co-constituting subjects because of the prophetic anointing they received in baptism. However, the *sensus fidei ecclesiae*—which is not identical to the *sensus fidei fidelium* because the church is more than the sum of the *fideles* who are its members—is also determined by the specific contribution made by "the preaching of those who have received a certain charism of truth," that is, the bishops (see DV 8), in order to maintain its apostolic roots. Faith in God is always interior, but it must be symbolized, communicated, and professed so that it builds up the church and keeps alive the dangerous memory of Jesus. Since there is always the risk of erroneous, partial, and falsified interpretations of the first Christian proclamation, the church can experience difficulties and conflicts in correctly interpreting the proclamation, and so it needs the discernment of those in the church who through the gift of the Spirit can guarantee the apostolicity of the faith.

The social construction of the ecclesial "We" takes place in an interpretative communicative medium[16] that involves all Christians and requires the specific contribution of the word of the bishops. Every transmission of constitutive meanings in the church reaffirms them and transforms them through the unique personal events of the individual subjects, and at the same time, it lives by the faith attested to as Christian and ecclesial because it is apostolic.

The statement of Vincent of Lerins remains central for defining the content of the *sensus fidei ecclesiae*: "We hold that faith which has been believed everywhere, always, by all."[17] Into this horizon LG 12 introduces a third concept, the *consensus fidelium*, and it outlines the dynamics that lead to the development of this *consensus* and the recognition of its existence.[18] First, the *consensus* is not already given from the start: it is not a question of giving "assent" to something already defined, which remains unchangeable in a crystallized form of expression. What is at stake is an essential ecclesial dynamic toward *consensus*, which must be encouraged and guaranteed first and foremost by the bishops, who are the guarantors and promoters of the process. The *consensus fidelium* conveys and expresses on a public, empirically observable level the *sensus fidei ecclesiae*:[19] it is therefore a true and proper *"locus theologicus."* This dynamic engages all the baptized, but in differentiated functions of testimony and interpretation of the *depositum fidei*; the interaction always has a synchronic and a diachronic reference. Different "hermeneutical subjectivities" are present in the church, and different functions sustain the life of the church as a hermeneutical community. As Cardinal Newman beautifully stated when tracing the path of ecclesial formation and mission, "Truth is to be found through a *conspiratio fidelium et pastorum*."[20]

As we shall see, the *ordained ministers* guarantee, across time and space, the apostolicity of the proclamation that makes the church the "church of Jesus." They work to maintain the identity of this subject in an apostolic dynamic that is both foundational and eschatological. The *laity*, for their part, have an identity that is not exhausted in an "exclusive" and "univocal" relationship with the Christian community; they urge the whole church to read the signs of the coming of the kingdom of God in human history, and they foster an interpretation of the gospel according to the signs of the times and in the pluralist language of the world's cultures. Their professional skills and their everyday experiences of faith (see LG 35) enrich the church's understanding of the Word of God with specific contributions that are needed for theological reflection, ecclesial life, and the development of doctrine.

THE CONTRIBUTION OF
THE MAGISTERIUM

The description of ecclesial life outlined in *Lumen Gentium* 12 offers helpful suggestions for understanding the specific role of the magisterium and for delineating the correct forms and boundaries of the relationship between magisterium and laity,[21] thus overcoming the exclusive (and sometimes exclusionary) centrality of the magisterium that has been asserted for centuries. The whole church mediates and transmits revelation in its various components, but the *sensus fidei* of the people of God does not arise independently of the exercise of the episcopal magisterium; indeed, it requires it. The people of God is indefectible and infallible in believing *and teaching* precisely because it includes ordained ministers *within it.*[22] Laypeople and ordained ministers collaborate in the search for truth; through a normative function that is reciprocal, critical, and complementary, they attain a recognition of the content of faith in the magisterium and the *sensus fidei fidelium.* There is a widespread feeling that the magisterium has been a "competitor" rather than a "partner" (to borrow the apt title of a collection of essays dedicated to the *sensus fidei*),[23] but the conciliar texts clearly affirm that the ministerial subject, to whom is assigned magisterial competence, resides in the responsible communion of all believers and is placed at its service. Indeed, the magisterium is expected to "listen, nourish, and receive" the *sensus fidei fidelium. Lumen Gentium* 12 portrays the bishops as guarantors of the ecclesial process leading to the *consensus fidelium*; they are guarantors of the *consensus* itself for the sake of the church's apostolicity. As Walter Kasper stated, the ecclesiastical magisterium serves the communication event of the ecclesial community; it must guarantee "an institutional space in which open and public dialogue is possible" because "the collective, dialogical discovery of the truth must be the normal, ordinary practice in the church."[24] As Yves Congar put it, "The whole church learns, and the whole church teaches, but in a differentiated manner."[25]

CONCLUSION

Recognition of the *sensus fidelium* constitutes the essential keystone for the realization of a synodal church,[26] which means a people endowed by the Spirit with a prophetic messianic mission and a hermeneutic community in which all members, ordained and lay, contribute with their individual charisms to an ever new and vital understanding of the gospel and to the development of Tradition. It is in this light that the subjectivity and the ministeriality of all the *christifideles* must be rethought. It is in this light that creativity and courage will point the ways to structural reform that will allow for the development of a synodal church characterized by co-sharing of faith and great pastoral synergy. For this process to take place, it will obviously be necessary to abandon the communications model that is most widespread in the church today, the unidirectional top-down and center-to-periphery model that moves from the clergy to the laity. The church must instead open itself to multidirectional communicational dynamics that shape the church as a synodal communion. "We must ensure that the riches of the *sensus fidei* can fully blossom and bear abundant fruit."[27]

3

The Pathways to
Renewed Ministries

During the pontificate of Pope Francis, the option for the model of synodal church has been progressively affirmed, enabling the implementation of the ecclesiological vision of a priestly, prophetic, and royal "people of God," as outlined in chapter II of the Constitution on the Church, *Lumen Gentium*. In accord with his usual style of work, Pope Francis first implemented the change on the level of practice by expanding the faithful's involvement in the preparatory phase of the Synod of Bishops and then by motivating and deepening the process in speeches and documents.[1] Both his address on the occasion of the fiftieth anniversary of the creation of the Synod of Bishops,[2] which defines it as an instrument serving the exercise of the Petrine primacy, and the apostolic constitution *Episcopalis Communio*[3] situate the Synod of Bishops within the broader movement of ecclesial synodality; these documents redefine not only the synod's contribution to the life of the church but also the ecclesial dynamics and the subjects involved. The timely, wide-ranging consultation of the church's different components, as occurred in the Synod on the Family and the Synod on Young People, is no longer viewed as a mere subsidiary phase prior to the assembly of the bishops in Rome. Listening to all the voices in the different local churches is now understood to be the first and indispensable phase of the synodal journey of the entire people of God. The celebration of the Synod of Bishops appears as part of that journey; it is an essential moment of episcopal discernment in service to the universal church so that the journey becomes inclusive and communal.[4]

MAKING CHURCH TOGETHER

Thinking of a church that recognizes itself and functions in a synodal way means shifting away from the secular biases in management authority and organizational dynamics; it calls for a recalibration of the participatory, communicative, formative, and decision-making dynamics by which the church "is and becomes church"; it demands a new recognition, *de jure* and *de facto*, of the contribution of all ecclesial subjects, from the laity to the bishop of Rome.[5] This unprecedented configuration of ecclesial relations will help the church, which has become global, to rediscover the form of ecclesial relations that characterized the first four centuries of its history.

The ecclesiological presuppositions of this shift are indicated in the constitutions on the church and on the liturgy and in the decrees *Ad Gentes, Christus Dominus,* and *Presbyterorum Ordinis.* According to these documents of Vatican II, all members of the church have equal dignity and are subjects co-constituting the church, albeit within the asymmetry that ordained ministry introduces into intra-ecclesial relations. All members of the church, in the diversity of their charisms and ministries, are co-responsible for the one messianic mission. The church has a communal essence that is generated by the gospel proclamation and is sustained by the multidirectional communicational dynamics that involves all ecclesial subjects. Vatican II offers an unprecedented reappraisal of the whole of the second millennium of church history as regards both the ordained ministry and the recognition and valorization of the laity. Regarding the ordained ministry, there is clearly a mature theology with a few unsettled questions, but regarding laypeople, there are very different visions that are not fully reconciled.

A synodal form of church develops in the polyphony of ecclesial voices,[6] in accord with a *con-spiratio* oriented to an ever deeper understanding of the gospel in history (see DV 10). The synodal form requires the synergy of both ordained ministers and laypeople, as stated in *Lumen Gentium* 30: *ut cuncti suo modo ad commune opus unanimiter cooperentur*, "that all collaborate together in the common work, each in their own way." Given this twofold trajectory, synodality functions by virtue of a vital correlation between, on the one hand, the prophetic and royal *munera* of all the *christifideles* and the whole people of God (which includes ordained ministers) and, on the other, the exercise of the *munera docendi, regendi ac pascendi* proper to bishops. The option made for a synodal form of church makes it possible to overcome the age-old division between *ecclesia docens* and *ecclesia discens* (the former being the active subject, the latter merely the recipient). Furthermore, synodality makes it possible to deconstruct at their roots both the hierarchical paradigm, which continues to influence, even unconsciously, our ideas of ecclesial relations, and the logic of the *cursus honorum* in the approach to ministries. Not only does synodality help us to conceive of church as "being and walking together" (the *syn-* prefix of the word *synod*), but it also allows an authentic interaction to take place among all subjects, thus producing a veritable "choreography" of ministerial actors.[7] The inclusion of new subjects (laity, women) in the process of understanding the faith and developing the Tradition induces all other subjects to resituate themselves in the ecclesial dynamics and to rethink their proper roles in the relationship, in this way rediscovering the logic of co-responsibility on the journey toward full maturity (see Eph 4:7–16).

Ministerial Reform

A synodal church is not possible, therefore, without a genuine and binding reconfiguration of ministry in the church.[8] In the long postconciliar season, the documents of Vatican II have been received in a way that has transformed the face of the local churches and the self-awareness of all those involved. In matters ranging from the dynamics of celebration to pastoral life in all its moments, both ordained ministers and laypeople have welcomed changes that have gone beyond the mere letter of the documents in many respects. At the same time, there has been much resistance to change, and there have been recurrent attempts to discourage fresh new developments in the church. The trajectory of magisterial hermeneutics in the postconciliar period regarding these issues is in some respects revealing:[9] on the one hand, there was a necessary consolidation to correct the ill-advised experimentation or illicit practices that had occurred in the first creative phase of postconciliar reception; on the other hand, there was an attempt to "delimit" the disruptive force of certain conciliar texts. From the mid-1980s onward, interpretations of ordained ministry based on a christological-sacerdotal foundation returned to the forefront, with an overemphasis on the priest's sacred character as what distinguishes him before the community. Meanwhile, little heed was given to the perspective on ministry recommended by the Council, which rested on an ecclesiological-pneumatological foundation.

In *Ministeria Quaedam*, Paul VI applied the term *ministry* to the laity for the first time, but John Paul II subsequently, in *Christifideles Laici* 23 and in the interdicasterial instruction *Ecclesiae de Mysterio*, considered such a use to be improper. He preferred to think of the laity's contribution in terms of "collaboration with the hierarchy" rather than in terms of authentic ecclesial co-responsibility.[10] Only with Pope Francis was there a return to the call for full ministeriality in the church, for the ministries of the laity, and for the co-responsibility of all the baptized.[11] The universal reception of the local churches is more vigorous and advanced than is evident from most official documents and most theological literature;[12] the most valuable witnesses to this reality are the magisterial documents of the national and continental bishops' conferences, the acts of the diocesan synods, and above all, the daily practice.

The Subjectuality of Laypeople

The postconciliar period has undoubtedly suffered from the weakness of Vatican II's reflections on the laity.[13] *Lumen Gentium* 4 and *Apostolicam Actuositatem* are the first documents in the history of the church dedicated to the laity and their contribution to the life of the church. After centuries in which the status of laypeople was underestimated and the word of the laity considered irrelevant for building up the ecclesial body, these documents do no more than express the best "theology of the laity" that was available in the 1950s. According to this theology, the pastors deliver the moral, spiritual, and religious principles that guide the laity in their apostolic work and Christian witness, and the laity, for their part, because of their secular nature (LG 31; AA 7), are called to "manage the things of the world according to God's will" and to "incarnate" the gospel and the Christian faith in society, in the family, and in the spheres of politics and work.

The Council Fathers went further when they proposed that laypeople have a specific role in formulating religious principles and in understanding the gospel (*Lumen Gentium* 2; *Gaudium et Spes* 43), but this teaching did not reach sufficient maturity. In any case, these two interpretations, which we could respectively define as a "theology of the laity" and a "theology of being laypeople," stay close to the texts and do not give rise to a thorough review of the identity of those who, as Pope Francis says, are "the immense majority of the church."[14] Moreover, the conciliar documents portray the many contributions of the laity to pastoral life, from catechesis to liturgical services to missionary work, as auxiliary and secondary in comparison to the contributions of the ordained ministers. The laity are sometimes said to offer their services "in an extraordinary form" or as a "substitute" in case of a shortage of clergy.[15] Today, however, church life all over the world, from associations to parishes to dioceses, is a totally different scenario, with widespread involvement of laypeople in all pastoral sectors.

The Challenge

To meet the challenge of synodality and synodal reform, we must ask some serious questions: What vision of the laity guides us? What new forms of lay ministry should be promoted? And how can we recognize the specific contribution that comes from women? Courageous reflection is required to implement fully the conciliar vision of ordained ministry—bishops, priests, and deacons—and to address the open questions concerning the appointment of bishops, the nature of leadership, the exercise of power, training in seminaries, the requirement of celibacy for priests in the Latin church, and cooperation with the laity. Finally, synodality demands reflection on a forgotten ministry, that of married couples. Every member of the community is the bearer of a specific word in the synodal church; each person carries out a singular, irreplaceable action for the synodal church.

"The concept of synodality refers to the co-responsibility and participation of the whole people of God in the life and mission of the church,"[16] but how do the different ecclesial subjects truly contribute to shaping and developing the synodal form of church, both at the local level (parishes and dioceses) and at the universal level? What resistance does the project of synodal reform face in its commitment to listening to all and acknowledging the subjectivity of all? How can ministry be reconfigured in the church so that the people of God in their journey through history can best avail themselves of the contributions of everyone?

LAYPEOPLE AS MEMBERS IN A SYNODAL CHURCH

The document of the International Theological Commission, *Synodality in the Life and Mission of the Church*, offers the broadest and best articulated reflection on the implementation of synodality in the different contexts and levels of ecclesial life, but it mentions the theme of the laity in only a few passages. These passages are nevertheless relevant for understanding the foundational assumptions and the hermeneutics of the conciliar documents, and they specify concretely the contribution required of the laity in a synodal church.[17] The horizon of reference is obviously the ecclesiology of Vatican II, especially its notions regarding the "people of God," the *sensus fidei ecclesiae/fidelium* (LG 12), and the laity's work of evangelizing and bearing prophetic witness in the world in service to the kingdom of God. In discussing synodality, we are asked to take a stand for one of the two theological interpretations present in the vision of Vatican II, namely, the one that recognizes the "co-essentiality of hierarchical and charismatic gifts"[18] and places in the foreground the subjectivity of the word that is rooted in baptism and charisms (LG 4, 7, 12).

This interpretation distances us from the more traditional one, which insists on the secular nature of the laity and their apostolate in the world. The laity are *synodoi*[19] (LG 55); that is, they are members co-constituting the collective church, "the ecclesial We," and their contribution is recognized as "indispensable" to the life of the church.[20] They are not to be seen as simply obedient executors of instructions given by clergy nor as mere collaborators in pastoral work for which they are not truly responsible. Nor should they be considered passive recipients of doctrinal formation that only ordained ministers can offer; rather, they possess a vision of reality and a spiritual experience that must be recognized and welcomed so that the work of evangelization and the life of the church can be fulfilled. In the synodal church two dynamics are at work, understanding the faith together and deciding together; both require cooperation and unity of purpose. On both planes the laity are to be understood as active members[21] with their own subjectivity of speech, with their own specific contribution to community discernment, and with autonomy around pastoral action. Only in this way does it become possible to implement what is stipulated in *Ad Gentes*:

> The church has not been really founded, and is not yet fully alive, nor is it a perfect sign of Christ among men and women unless there is a laity worthy of the name working along with the hierarchy. For the Gospel

cannot be deeply grounded in the abilities, life, and work of any people without the active presence of lay people. Therefore, even at the very founding of a Church, great attention is to be paid to establishing a mature, Christian laity.[22]

Understanding the Faith Together and Deciding Together

A synodal church is generated and regenerated by the Word of the Gospel heard and understood ever more deeply thanks to the word of all the *christifideles* who constitute the church. While the ordained ministers guarantee the apostolicity of the proclamation and of the church (see LG 18, 24), the laity invite everyone to grasp the coming of God in the history of humanity, thus preserving the extroversion and secularity of the whole church,[23] its being in the world and for the world (its pro-existence). Their word of faith is shaped by laypeople's professional skills, their family experiences, and their active involvement in politics, economics, and culture. During synodal meetings and in pastoral councils, laypeople read the signs of the times (see GS 4) and communicate the gospel proclamation using the language of their time (see GS 44) so that its scope and meaning can be understood today. Precisely because of their contribution to the hermeneutics of the gospel and the *Traditio Ecclesiae* (see DV 8), the laity ensure that the commitment to synodality is not reduced to an intra-ecclesial retreat but remains constitutively open to mission.

We understand the gospel with the help of the languages of our time, and we understand the extent and the shape of the ecclesial mission in the light of the promise of the kingdom we serve together, the kingdom of God coming in history. Thanks to their experience in the civil and political spheres—trade unions, citizens' associations, voluntary work, and so on—laypeople can make specific contributions to shaping the synodal church. Precisely because they are accustomed to democratic and participatory procedures and to cooperative forms of social organization, they can contribute to rethinking internal relations within the ecclesial body, especially regarding the exercise of authority, the distinction of powers, the greater involvement of women, and the dynamics of communication and information. Such rethinking in the church will lead to increased transparency, accountability, and representativity and to more effective community action.

Sixty years after the Second Vatican Council, there is today no way that lay involvement can be disregarded or stealthily limited. Before making an authoritative pronouncement, the bishops (and the priests as well) should "listen to, nurture, and receive" what the laity have to contribute from their wisdom, competence, and experience of life, and they should do so without paternalism and in a spirit of real dialogue.[24] The relevance of the contribution of the laity to the life of the church is affirmed in canon 212 of the Code of Canon Law, according to which the faithful have not only the right to make their needs known to the pastors, but also the right and the duty to express their opinions on what is good for the church to the pastors and to the other faithful as well.[25] This latter reference reveals the possibility of thinking about "public opinion" in the church.

The contribution of the laity is indispensable in community discernment and in deliberative processes, precisely because it introduces "other" languages, categories, questions, and perspectives to the understanding of reality. Moreover, it makes operational alternatives possible, and it allows for the evaluation of pastoral options and their possible repercussions. "Synodality is not only a group of people walking together toward a common goal; it is a community trying to find a way together through collective discernment."[26] Despite these important considerations, the contribution of the laity, who constitute the majority of the faithful, is still limited to offering "advice to the pastors" that is at best useful, but not necessary or binding.[27]

The reduced space allowed for the laity to speak, the limited time given to listening to their concerns in the parishes, the concentration of all major decisions in the hands of ordained ministers alone, the little effort put into making participative bodies effective and efficient, the limited resources (in terms of people and financial commitment) invested in the formation of the laity, and the inability to accept the prophetic word of young people who are calling for substantial reforms in today's church—all these are signs of a failure to achieve the synodality that is essential for true church renewal.

The membership of the laity is always diverse; it is never reducible to a singular abstract "layperson" or to an undifferentiated category such as "laity." Recognizing this membership as essential to a synodal church concretely means welcoming the voices that have remained "unheard" for centuries: young people, women, the poor, and the marginalized—even those "dissonant" voices that are sometimes critical but are necessary for considering the life of the church from a different perspective and for overcoming the "same old, same old" that forever perpetuates itself. The authoritative heft of the laity is still limited; their power is evanescent, generic, and irrelevant; it is the result of limited, benevolent concessions from above, but it is not structurally integrated into the processes of ecclesial listening. Listening to the Word of God through the words of our brothers and sisters in the faith, and listening to each other's opinions, even contrasting ones, so that together they can produce mature church decisions—these are the essential ways of building a synodal church. It cannot be achieved unless the laity are recognized as true members.

Toward an "All-Ministerial Church"

Laypersons therefore help the synodal church to mature by working in the diverse contexts and activities of pastoral life. Since Vatican II, all the local churches have, in different ways, witnessed the flourishing of various forms of lay ministry, and these have radically transformed the face of the Christian community.[28] This is one of the most significant changes in the life of the church. Laymen and -women are actively involved in many forms of significant and ongoing service to the church; they have been given a specific mandate to respond to the pastoral and other needs of people and the region. Some who receive special training receive a special mandate from the bishop to be the heads of diocesan pastoral offices; they become pastoral officers, engaged full-time in the life of the parishes and other diocesan organizations.[29] Other laypeople serve as community coordinators in the absence of a priest, and they provide pastoral care as established by canon 512 §2 of the Code of Canon Law.[30]

In 1972, Paul VI, with the motu proprio *Ministeria Quaedam*, established what today we call "instituted ministries."[31] Lectors and acolytes are ancient ministerial figures who today assume a specific task of service on the basis of their baptism and a "specific rite of institution"; they nourish a fruitful relationship between the celebration of the Eucharist and the pastoral life of the faithful. Paul VI reserved these ministries to males only, by "venerable tradition," but Pope Francis has opened them up also to women and has promoted a further instituted ministry, that of the catechist.[32] These measures are not simply ratifying *de facto* tasks and ministries; they are creating new ministerial figures. Their existence disrupts the "clergy/laity" duality that has served as a matrix for past thinking about ecclesial relations, and it allows for the consideration of a multiplicity of ministerial figures: ordained, instituted, and *de facto*. The forms of ministry exercised by lay-people in and for the church are diverse: on the one hand, there are *de facto* ministries that are carried out for limited times and contexts; on the other, there are instituted ministries that entail enlivening other laypeople; these are taken on *permanently* in a local church after suitable training.

All these ministries are an indispensable contribution to the structure and action of the church, not only because clergy may be scarce, but also because laypeople are recognized as co-responsible members in the church. From the 1990s onward, certain suspicions and warnings were voiced about using the term *ministry* for the laity, but Francis has restored legitimacy to this discourse and has given constituent value to lay contributions.

The Second Vatican Council offered only a partial vision regarding the ministry of "all" in the church; it did not use the term *ministry* for laypeople but insisted rather on their apostolate in the world, whether as individuals or in associations. Even when the Council mentions lay pastoral service (as in LG 33, 37; AA 20, 22), it considers it something "extraordinary." The weakness of the conciliar documents' reflection on the royal *munus* is especially evident when it comes to the laity, who are not expressly mentioned in chapter II of *Lumen Gentium* and who are referred to in chapter IV only as acting *ad extra*, in accord with their secular nature.[33] *Lumen Gentium* 36 makes no direct mention of the laity's contribution to ecclesial service, nor is there any mention of the laity's exercise of authority in the church by virtue of their specific royal *munus*. *Lumen Gentium* 37 describes the relationship between hierarchy and laity, but always with a clear distinction between *ad intra* and *ad extra*, between the clergy's full membership in the church and the laity's role as "collaborators."

The synodal form of church entails not only the exercise of the *munus regendi ac pascendi* of the ordained ministers (the "one"), but also the synergetic contribution of "all" and "some" (pastoral workers, in this case) in that common service that expresses and implements the royal *munus* of all baptized laypersons. The Council, however, not only separated the membership of ordained ministers and that of the laity but also referred to the *munus* of each of them with different foundations and orientations. According to the *Relatio*, the term is not used in the second chapter of the Dogmatic Constitution on the Church "because it would be difficult to devise a treatment of the governing function that would be compatible with both categories at the same time."[34] Since 1983, however, the Code of Canon Law has provided for some forms of lay participation in the exercise of government, with specific tasks in the diocesan and Roman curias, in the area of administration (chancellor, bursar, notary, censor) and in judiciary functions (all roles are possible except those of the judicial vicar and the single judge).[35] Is it possible to extend the reflection on this matter? For example, is it possible to think about the participation of the laity in the process of appointing bishops and parish priests? Could the laity take on roles of coordination, administration, and legal representation of parishes? What should be the basis of lay authority, and how should it be conceived? Such questions naturally flow from the reconfiguration of lay ministry in a synodal perspective.

Synodal Reform and Ministerial Reform

There can be no synodal reform unless we rethink the individual identities of the ecclesial subjects; their relations of reciprocity, recognition, and cooperation; and the basis of their authority. In its Final Document,[36] the Synod for Amazonia recalled the formula "all-ministerial Church," which was coined by Yves Congar in the early 1970s.[37] While not free of ambiguity—should everyone carry out a ministerial service in the local church to which they belong?—the expression certainly projects an ideal horizon of community life, one in which everyone assumes a smaller or larger task for the building up of the church, as called for in Ephesians 4:7–16.

There can be no synodal reform without a corresponding ministerial reform, which must be carried out simultaneously and collaboratively by both ordained ministers and laity. Rethinking the relations between ministries based on baptism and the mandate of a bishop or a parish priest today requires both an attentive reading of the signs of the times and an exercise in creativity. It entails envisaging the future face of a church that can carry out its mission with the awareness that the ministries of the laity always have a constitutive extroverted perspective, even when serving the ecclesial body. A global church, confronted with many challenges on continents with diverse "organizational cultures," must develop diversified ministerial figures that can respond appropriately to the life of the local churches.[38] Such a development would allow the church to overcome the standardizing logic typical of the Tridentine model.

The experience of the Pan-Amazonian Synod is extremely interesting in this regard. Its Final Document suggested that laypeople be appointed to ministerial positions such as "custodians of the forest," "promoters of care for our common home," "community leaders," and "official welcomers of migrants arriving in the city."[39] In *Querida Amazonia*, the pope himself called for the development of a church in this region with a "markedly lay character," stating that the "capillary presence of the church" will be possible "*only* through the incisive protagonism of the laity."[40]

Progress toward a diaconal, synodal, and participatory church requires ongoing debate on the issue of ministries as well as reflection on existing innovative practices that already see the laity as protagonists and promoters of synodal communities, especially in places where there are few clergy, such as Latin America and Europe. Laypeople possess the creative ability to promote experiences that anticipate the future. Precisely because the "goal is to build a participatory church,"[41] the rethinking of ministries is not just a matter of greater efficiency or of redistribution of powers in the ecclesial body, such that space is given to those previously neglected. Every ministry has a functional and a symbolic dimension. It is the face of the church shaped by the way its ministry is exercised and by the style and dynamics of the service rendered: manifold ministry is now ordinary in the life of dioceses and parishes.

WOMEN, THE UNHEARD VOICE IN THE CHURCH

The Preparatory Document for the 2021–23 Synod, addressing the need to promote inclusion and dialogue in the church, refers to two women, the Canaanite and the Samaritan, and it affirms, "Jesus accepts as interlocutors all those who come from the crowd." These are the only two explicit references to women in the document, although it is clear that women must be included in everything that concerns laypeople and religious. Similarly, in the International Theological Commission's document *Synodality in the Life and Mission of the Church*, we find only two brief explicit references to the participation of baptized women in the life of the church and to the competent contribution they can make (105, 109d); there are also four generic references to "men and women."

What do the words and actions of women signify for the understanding and development of an authentic synodality?[42] This question is undoubtedly central to the reform of the church, for it emerges in every context—from diocesan synods to pastoral councils, from the German Synodal Way to the Amazon Synod—in which women contribute to reflection on the future of the church, bringing their own experience and delineating the serious challenges. Since the beginning of his pontificate, Pope Francis has been particularly attentive to and aware of the issue of women, and he has urged the church to listen to the just claims for women's rights because of the challenges and questions they pose to the whole church.[43] What is at stake today is proper recognition of women, after centuries of marginalization and undervaluation in the life of the church (albeit with some splendid and memorable exceptions, such as Hildegard of Bingen, Teresa of Avila, Catherine of Siena, and others). Indeed, what is at stake is nothing less than the effective proclamation of the gospel and the prophetic witness of the church itself.

The Vision of Vatican II

Reflection on the contribution of women to a synodal church finds light in Vatican II, both in the event itself and in its ecclesiology of the people of God, as outlined, above all, in *Lumen Gentium*.[44] For the first time in the second millennium, twenty-three women auditors, both religious and lay, participated in the work of the Council during its third and fourth sessions. It was Cardinal Suenens who, together with some male auditors and a few bishops, had asked for the presence of women. The women contributed significantly to the work of the commissions and were always available for consultation, but they were never allowed to speak in the council hall. Nonetheless, many elements since the Council—the vision of the church as the people of God, the recovery of the subjectivity of the laity in the church based on their baptism, and the reading of that great sign of the times that is the entry of women into political, social, and economic life—have led to the affirmation and recognition of the subjectivity of women in churches all over the world.

The change that took place is undeniable, and it has obvious repercussions on our understanding of synodal dynamics: as noted earlier, since Vatican II, the subjectivity of public, competent, and authoritative speech of women has become more recognized. Mothers and grandmothers have always passed on the faith and educated their children and grandchildren in the experience of Christian life, and women religious have offered the church the faithful word of prayer and wisdom. For centuries, however, the word of women believers remained confined and delimited within the spaces of the home, the monastery, and the convent. Women in the church[45] were faithful listeners, but they were also the subjects of "unheard words." Their voices were not heard in the aisles of the churches, in the public square, or in the university lecture halls in which theology and morals were debated. They were not recognized as bearers of an essential and constitutive element for the construction of the ecclesial member. In a church that considered itself to be "neutral" with regard to the differences between the sexes, the presence of women, always faithful and generous, was considered as something "obvious." For centuries, women were "the forgotten partners,"[46] the "invisible subjects," though they were always present and active.

The great shift brought about by the Council was prepared for throughout the nineteenth century by the extraordinary development of women's associations and women's religious life. In those contexts, women began to form themselves and to experience autonomous management in work, voting, and ecclesiastical service. There is no doubt, however, that the Council gave women words with which to speak for themselves as women and as believers; to express themselves in the denied language of theology. Women's words are increasingly being recognized in ecclesial life as meaningful and authoritative, especially in the everyday contexts of community life such as parishes, dioceses, and lay associations and movements. The transformative role of women reinvigorates the entire ecclesial structure, and it derives precisely from this new public recognition of their competent discourse as a valuable resource for developing further and more profound changes.

The word of women has shaped the postconciliar church[47] in countless ways: in the proclamation of the faith; in the pastoral services in which women's *diakonia* has been realized; in all the local churches; in the renewal of religious life; in the word of the women theologians who, after Vatican II, began to study and teach in the pontifical universities; and in the various roles of responsibility they have assumed (especially in the last two decades) in the Roman Curia, in dioceses, and in national pastoral offices. Now that the recognition of a membership proper to women is emerging in the ecclesial sphere (long after it happened in civil society and in most cultures), the synodal church must be conceived of as a church of "men and women," and the remaining cultural and structural resistances to women's speech must be overcome. It is not enough to talk about women or to women, nor is it enough to discuss women's issues, isolating them from the rest of ecclesial reform. The task now is to activate synodal dynamics and to consider from a synodal perspective the changes that are needed. This task involves listening to all those involved—first, women with their questions, challenges, desires, efforts, and experiences—while recognizing all subjectualities or memberships (those of men and women as partners) and projecting an inclusive, just, and participatory ecclesial face.

A Church of Men and Women

In a truly synodal church, without prejudice to the specificity of charisms and ministries, the contribution of all members is rooted in the recognition of their equal dignity and common responsibility by virtue of being baptized, as affirmed in Galatians 3:28 ("There is no longer male *and* female; for all of you are one in Christ Jesus").[48] We walk together in a communion that is born and nourished by the communication of faith, where everyone is a co-constituent member and the bearer of a unique and irreplaceable word. First, women remember that each person's experience of faith is uniquely "incarnated" and that the words of witness and understanding of the gospel that are proclaimed and shared by all are marked by the undeniable and irrepressible difference of gender. A church that sets out on a synodal path must create the conditions, the times, and the structures for true listening and dialogue so that the contributions of men and women are recognized regardless of gender.

A synodal church must go beyond facile stereotypes that reduce "women" (as members) to ideas of "feminine values" and spousal-maternal femininity, thus forgetting cultural differences and the specificity of lived experiences. There is therefore a need to tackle the taboo questions of masculinity in the Catholic Church and the relationship between masculinity and sacred power; these issues have so far been given little consideration in theology and are practically ignored in preaching and catechesis. Theological anthropology is immature and incomplete when it conceives of the human being (*anthropos*) as a universalized neutral "male" (*aner*) and then, in a second act, tries to define the "specificity of the female." Thinking as a synodal church involves resolving this question of the relationships between men and women, which are neither of subordination nor of simple complementarity of male and female; rather, men and women are related in a partnership of believing members. It is time to think of ourselves as "brothers and sisters" or "believing men and women," thus going beyond the imaginary "maternal" and "spousal" projections whereby men entrust themselves to women and their love.[49] There is an urgent need today to overcome this biased vision, which is based on a Marian archetype, as in John Paul II's *Mulieris Dignitatem* (1988), or else on a comparison between a Petrine principle and a Marian principle, which may be of Balthasarian origin but is not biblically founded.[50]

The church is an institution that is "gender-structured," but it does not consciously recognize itself as such. The liturgies and languages used for celebrating the faith are still apparently neutral,[51] and theology has not been rethought from a gender perspective. Catechesis and the teaching of the Catholic religion are conducted without paying attention to the issues of sexual difference. In these areas, the words of women and men, through synodal dialogue, must contribute to changes that cannot be postponed without seriously weakening the proclamation of the faith and the life of the church.

Beyond Hierarchical Logic

The second word of criticism and renewal that women offer the church concerns the form of ecclesial relations.[52] A synodal church flourishes through the constitutive relationship—in terms of communication, participation, and decisions—between "one," "some," and "all," as the document of the International Theological Commission reminds us. Nevertheless, the Catholic Church remains in some respects a "kyriarchical" system (to use Elisabeth Schüssler Fiorenza's term):[53] it is centered on the logic of the *kyrios*, of the "one" lord, who exercises power *over* everybody (all women and many men). Making the church synodal requires not only including women, as a disadvantaged group, in the many contexts of pastoral life, but also working to change the relations among all members. Such a change involves overcoming the clerical-masculine culture, discarding the patriarchal structure, and dismantling a system of "hierarchical" logic that lacks accountability and adequate transparency in decision-making.[54]

This will undoubtedly entail enhancing the contribution of women to the church's ministry, not only the many *de facto* ministries they now perform but also the instituted ministries of Reader, Acolyte, and Catechist. Ideological and structural resistance to the exercise of women's subjectivity and ministry must be opposed. Women who are pastoral workers encounter chronic sexism and "benevolent patriarchy" daily that reveal a deep-rooted clerical mentality. Glass ceilings and fences (vertical and horizontal gender barriers that are quite difficult to breach) prevent the church from enjoying the valuable contributions of women to decision-making processes and leadership tasks. The resistance even to discussing the issue of women voting in synods (at least where it is possible, as at the diocesan level, in my opinion, but not during the assembly of the Synod of Bishops proper) is an indication of a general unwillingness to recognize women's authority and management capability. Women do not at the present time define the "symbolic reference systems" for the ecclesial body as a whole, except indirectly by forming men who will have ecclesial power or by affecting individual sectors or fields of activity with well-defined boundaries, as a sort of "male concession."

Women denounce the gender gap, which wounds the church deeply, and call for official recognition of the women's leadership that already exists in grassroots contexts—for example, by creating in Latin America the established ministry of "grassroots community leader or coordinator." Women also call for discussion about women's roles in other types of ministries, such as preaching homilies and exercising pastoral authority.[55] Many theologians hold that the ordination of women as deacons is possible based on Vatican II's theology of ministry,[56] and it is supported by hundreds of historical and theological studies. Moreover, it has been requested by many bishops' conferences and diocesan synods, as well as by the Amazon Synod. The ordination of women deacons would preserve the apostolicity of the faith and would strengthen the ecclesial "We"—the church—in those communities that have no priest or are far from the parish church, and it would undoubtedly change the "exclusively masculine" style in which power is perceived and exercised.

Promoting synodality as a *modus vivendi et operandi ecclesiae* entails rethinking deliberative processes and the dynamics of communication; it touches on the theme of power as well as on the theme of the relations between the "one" (always male), the "some" (pastoral workers, theologians), and the "all." Synodality, therefore, requires considerable reflection on ecclesial subjects, the types of ministries, and the ordained ministry. This reflection cannot happen unless we take seriously the debate and the research on the theme of women's ordination and courageously reclaim the ancient Tradition and the New Testament testimonies on female ministerial figures.

The Ways of Ecclesial Regeneration

The changes that have taken place in the postconciliar church are unquestionable, but other steps need to be taken in terms of pastoral conversion, the culture of recognition, and structural reform. There is need for change in many structures and practices, including educational, decision-making, and participatory systems; pastoral activities and language usage; the training of clergy; and the integration of women into theological faculties.[57]

The fundamental resource in a synodal church is precisely the "word," and the word always has a cognitive dimension. The word gives birth to thought, which becomes voice, sharing, transmission of ideas, motivation, and reason. The word is testimony; it narrates the events in which one has been a protagonist and on which one has reflected. Such events can lead to denunciation because they violate the dignity of women, or they can appear as positive anticipations of the future dreamed of. The word is communication that weaves together relationships amid differences, differences that are revealed and therefore understood. The word starts "from oneself" and goes forth to meet others and to come together to generate the "We." The word can evoke a future that does not yet exist and thus open new paths.[58] The word makes it possible to reaffirm what already exists—to make it visible and real for all—and at the same time to denounce the gender gap, the absence of women, the culpable exclusions, the silence imposed on so many. And when words are muted and being heard seems impossible, there remains the space of the symbol, of the silent, nonviolent appeal.[59]

In a synodal church, the focus is on listening together to the Word of God, heard through the word of one and all, and on examining the relations between men and women to transform unequal relationships and structures so as to allow all to share in the variety of differences, according to the evangelical project of the kingdom of God. Innovative experiences must be narrated so that others will realize that it is licit and possible for women to take on roles of authority. Exegetical and theological works written by women must be disseminated and debated; the testimonies of female figures from the scriptures and church history must motivate spiritual change and inspire the courage to speak out. In a synodal church, the challenge is to speak "new languages," to speak the language of women, to speak *to* women, and to speak *as* women who understand the gospel and proclaim it. As Michelle Rosaldo states, "The place of women is decided not by what they do, but on the basis of what their activities mean in the concrete social institution."[60] Therefore, no church will be synodal if the competent, public, authoritative word does not have conditions and spaces in which to resonate and be accepted as an essential, constitutive word for creating church by understanding the faith together and by deciding together for the common good. Nor will the church be synodal if ecclesial relations are not thoroughly rethought from a gender perspective, so as to overcome the clerical-masculine culture and the patriarchal structure. Those who in this dynamic process fail to recognize one of the partners—the one that is, in fact, the most active at the ecclesial base and the most significant for the changes that have taken place on the sociocultural level—will end up weakening, blocking, and ultimately rendering impossible any transformative dynamic in a synodal key.

> An excessively fearful and structured Church will be constantly critical of all discourse defending women's rights and will constantly point out the risks and possible errors of such claims. Conversely, a dynamic Church will react by paying attention to women's legitimate claims for more justice and equality. It will study history and recognize a long pattern of male authoritarianism, subjugation, and various forms of slavery, abuse, and male violence. With this perspective, the church will be able to make these claims for women's rights its own, and even if it does not agree with everything that some feminist groups propose, it will make its own wholehearted contribution to greater reciprocity between men and women. Accordingly, the Synod wished to

renew the Church's commitment to fighting "against all discrimination and violence with a sexual basis."[61]

THE MINISTRY OF COUPLES

In rethinking the form of the synodal church, it is also important to approach the ministry of couples united by the sacrament of marriage.[62] This theme has received little attention in ecclesiology or in pastoral and sacramental studies. Spouses are rarely told of their ministerial responsibility as a couple; mention is made only of their membership as ministers in the celebration of the sacrament. To reconfigure a synodal church, reference must be made to the specific contribution of the married couple's word and presence, for they attest to and safeguard the communal form of being church in a special way.[63]

The Prophecy of Communion in Difference

Marriage and the life of the couple are today, especially in the West, undergoing a profound transformation, with a significant reshaping of roles. The reasons for uniting in marriage are less linked to procreation than in the past; priority is given instead to the affective dimension and the communicational dynamics in the couple. These aspects are recognized as constitutive of a relationship of love and communion that aspires to the ideal of equal dignity and reciprocity between man and woman. The family is first and foremost seen as a "place of affection," a "community of life and relationships." Marriage is chosen based on shared intimacy and the joint elaboration of projects, expectations, and norms; there is less stress on the juridical-contractual aspect: "The cohesion factor assumed by the couple is based on the priority of the affective dimension over the contractual agreement and the objective regulation of the commitment" (A. Melloni). As *Gaudium et Spes* states, the family is "an intimate community of life and conjugal love," established "on the covenant between the spouses, that is, on their irrevocable personal consent" (GS 48). Pope Francis emphasizes this perspective in *Amoris Laetitia*.

The sacrament of marriage, far from being simply the institutionalized ratification of the natural and social union of a man and a woman, is an ecclesial act. Two baptized persons, who are already members of the ecclesial body, recognize that they are participants *together* in God's historical engagement with humanity, and they therefore decide to celebrate—as their own ministers—their union as a revelatory and actualizing part of God's *mysterion* in Christ (see Ephesians 5). A historical-personalist reading of the sacrament of matrimony (which is not limited to the moment of the celebration, but considers the subjects and the lasting dynamics that are generated) and an eschatological-ecclesial vision of matrimonial relations[64] will help us to grasp the fact that every matrimonial union is already in itself a communion in difference and a physical and social sign of love and covenant (which Christians always recognize as a mediation of God's grace), and that consequently the union of those who "marry...in the Lord" (1 Cor 7:39) generates a new ecclesial membership for the couple and gives them a singular way of participating in the church's messianic mission.[65]

The sacrament makes the couple capable of enjoying the *charis* of God with humanity, and they do so precisely as a couple, reciprocally, as mediators with and for each other. The sacrament makes them participants in the church's mission in a new way, no longer individually, but as a "We," a "singular plural being" (to use J. L. Nancy's apt expression). In the ritually expressed consent and in their sexual union, an assertive act of mutual, reciprocal *traditio-receptio* is performed by these two sexually determined human subjects, and a new historical member, the couple, is generated from the two existences thus "co-expressed." Their communal relationship of reciprocity, which arises from the most radical and irreducible of the differences inscribed in the human being, the difference of sex/gender, becomes a living word that proclaims the nature of God's kingdom and the form of the church. As a couple, spouses enjoy trinitarian love, which pervades their relationship; thanks to the visibility of their relational dynamics, they are a privileged space for the manifestation of communion with God and among persons, the true essence of God's kingdom and the vital nature of the church. Spouses have a specific word to offer the church and the world, on the level both of sign and effective action—they attest to the unity in difference (that of gender) that love makes overflow with new life.

Beyond the Christian and ecclesial services performed by couples (such as evangelization of children; hospitality and opening their home to those in need; support for families in difficulty; *ministerium vitae* in procreating children, adoption of abandoned children, and education of new generations), what remains primary for the married couple is this word of the two becoming "one flesh," thus bearing witness in everyday life to the logic of love, communication, and communion in difference. When two members of the church perform this celebratory act, they take on a new role as a couple—the only form of ministry not entrusted to an individual. The whole church is affected by this act by which it realizes its communal essence and is reconfigured through the contribution of these new subjects who have become one flesh and participate in communion and in the ecclesial mission in a new way.

A Synodal Church Listening to Couples

By their simple existence, even more than by their actions, the married couple bears witness to the values, the constituent elements, and the founding instances of communion. The couple is a living appeal to the church to recognize the value of sharing and co-responsibility; it is a custodian of difference and a critic of every logic of uniformity and regimentation; it is an affirmation that unity can never result from passive subordination to the authority of "one." These are the main elements of a synodal style, and they are the steps that must be taken if synodal conversion is to mature. Spouses remind a church that is committed to a synodal form of life that the mediation of the other, in its radical otherness, is necessary for authentic human maturation. They recall the fruitfulness that springs from an encounter in difference; they bear witness that time is a constitutive element of every human relationship and that the maturating of relationships requires the patience of constant confrontation. They bring the nature of the priesthood back to its existential form of *agapé*, exercised in the daily giving and receiving of oneself, and they point to the eschatological depths of the communal relationships that we form and by which we are formed. A church that seeks to be synodal can learn from spouses the value of both the daily dialogue that shapes relationships and the difficult wisdom of building unity by addressing conflicts without sublimating or hiding them.

The Council defines the family analogously as a "small church" or a "domestic church" (LG 11; AA 11).[66] Homes are ecclesial places for building up the synodal church: here, the specific ministry of spouses is to bear witness on the level of sign and to contribute on the level of loving practice to the promotion of the synodal church. It is therefore essential for parishes and dioceses to create opportunities for hearing and heeding the words of spouses, especially when they are seeking to forge unity in the face of conflict, when they are seeking to build consensus by respecting existing differences, or when they are seeking to open up pastoral life to the everyday spaces already marked by the presence of the God of life, spaces that the traditional categories of theology and clerical preaching often fail to appreciate.

THE ORDAINED MINISTRY

The guidelines that have emerged during the pontificate of Pope Francis have led to a reconsideration of the Synod of Bishops and a reframing of collegiality within the synodality of the whole church. Thus, the option for a synodal church necessarily entails a reappraisal of the way in which the ordained ministry is exercised in its three degrees, but it is particularly the case with the episcopate, which is the true driving force behind synodality at all levels of the church, from the local churches to the regional, the national, the continental, and finally the *communio ecclesiarum*.[67]

The theological assumptions underlying the vision of *Episcopalis Communio* can be found in the third chapter of *Lumen Gentium* and in the decrees of Vatican II dedicated to bishops and priests (*Christus Dominus, Presbyterorum Ordinis*). The International Theological Commission outlines in a more articulate and extensive manner the specific tasks, responsibilities, rights, and duties by which bishops and other ministers can develop synodal awareness and promote a synodal *modus vivendi et operandi* that is both effective and appropriate to the church's communal nature.

In the ongoing task of receiving the Council, many questions concerning ordained ministry appear unresolved, especially on the level of concrete pastoral practice. There is still not full acceptance of an ecclesiological vision that begins by considering local churches instead of taking the universal church as the main perspective for thinking about church. There is debate about the intermediate instances needed for a collegiality that is not only affective but also effective, starting with the episcopal conferences. More discussion is needed regarding the relationship between priests and their bishop and the role of the presbyterate in a diocese. More generally, greater clarity is needed, as the International Theological Commission observes (see no. 117), regarding such matters as the specificity of the diaconate, the relationship between the contribution of the people of God to the life of the church and the *sensus fidei*, and finally the exercise of authority, both on the level of magisterium and on the level of governance. Moreover, the Synod for the Amazon and various national synodal processes (Ireland, Australia, Germany) have made specific demands that would transform the exercise of ministry and the configuration of church life; these include ordaining married men to the priesthood, not requiring celibacy for priesthood, ordaining women as permanent deacons (and as priests), separating the formation of clergy from seminaries, involving the people of God in the appointment of bishops and parish priests, and overcoming individualistic forms of exercising pastoral ministry by promoting the establishment of pastoral teams.

The inculturation of ministerial forms in a globalized church requires bishops and priests to assume roles that are less sacralized and more capable of responding positively to the demands arising from the context of advanced secularization. The figure of the "Tridentine priest" as a "bulwark of solid doctrine" ends up being significant only for those who want the ecclesial experience to give them a sense of security in the face of the fluid complexity of the postmodern world. If we are to make the synodal church a reality, the great challenge is precisely that of developing a vision of ministry in Tradition that relates to current needs and modern forms of exercising leadership; such a vision recovers the ecclesiological-functional perspective of Vatican II, thus moving beyond the reductionist christological-sacerdotal interpretations of the 1990s. Systematic theology and practical theology are currently engaging each other in all geographical contexts, searching for new categories, models, and figures of ordained ministry. The topic is increasingly urgent and cannot be postponed, despite the resistance of many who opposed the ordination of women deacons and who champion the causes of celibacy and the sacred eucharistic *potestas* to slow down the reform that many faithful demand and perceive as necessary in the face of abuse, the identity crisis of priests, and weak episcopal leadership.

The guiding principle of reform consists of overcoming the Gregorian-Tridentine model of the church, which is centripetally centered on sacramentalization and structured around the ministry of priests and the *cura animarum* in which they are the protagonists. Such a model is static because it is designed to preserve the faith without ever leading to anything but slow changes. Adopting a synodal praxis requires overcoming this model and developing a new way forward, starting with the question of what specific contribution of word and authority is proper to the bishops, priests, and deacons in the local church, and situating their subjectivity in the overall synodal dynamic of ecclesial reconfiguration.

The Bishop in the Local Church

The recognition of the sacramentality of the episcopate (see LG 21) is one of the most significant elements of the ecclesiological renewal implemented by Vatican II;[68] it is a step with significant implications for the ecclesial model.[69] In a synodal church the role of the bishop is decisive and strategically central: the bishop is the guarantor of the apostolicity of the faith and of the catholicity of the church in which he serves as the "principle and foundation of unity." The bishop is charged with implementing synodality at all levels and in all contexts. In the synodal church, "the bishop is both teacher and disciple. He is a teacher when, endowed with the special assistance of the Holy Spirit, he proclaims to the faithful the word of truth in the name of Christ, head and shepherd. But he is a disciple when, knowing that the Spirit has been bestowed upon every baptized person, he listens to the voice of Christ speaking through the entire People of God."[70] In the communicative dynamic of dialogue, which is the framework of every event and every realization of synodality, the bishop is invited, first, to assume an attitude of listening and to create the conditions in which all the components of the ecclesial body can be heard. The document of the International Theological Commission mentions this basic aspect of the bishop's pastoral ministry several times. Second, the bishop exercises his specific *munus docendi* (LG 25) and his *munus regendi ac pascendi* (LG 27) by using community discernment.[71]

Drawing on magisterial and other authoritative teaching, he points out the indispensable elements of the apostolic faith and indicates the pastoral decisions that best express the nature of the church and its mission. In this way, he guides and directs the people of God on their path, always preserving the "ecclesial We"— the church—over which he is called to preside. "There is to be no distance or separation between the community and its Pastors… but [only] a distinction between tasks in the reciprocity of communion. A synod, an assembly, a council cannot take decisions without its legitimate Pastors."[72] The bishop is the promoter and the guarantor of the process leading to the *consensus fidelium* (LG 12), and to him is entrusted the public pronouncement of what has matured in the process of discernment (LG 25). At the same time, he is the one who guards the unity of the church through discernment of the charisms given by the Spirit and through nourishment of the synergy among all, *ut cuncti suo modo ad commune opus unanimiter cooperentur* (LG 30). For a widespread synodal consciousness to mature, the entire community must experience a profound pastoral conversion that recognizes the constitutive ministry of service of the "one" who presides over and safeguards the identity of the "We" in its apostolic roots, but the pastor's identity must also mature, so that he becomes capable of promoting forms and processes that are truly synodal in the local church entrusted to him. There is also a need for changes of those secular practices that do not allow a synodal *forma ecclesiae* to develop or that delay its realization. Two principal lines of action appear urgent, as reflected in the two expressions with which the bishop's identity was presented in the ancient tradition: *episcopus in ecclesia* and *episcopus pater populi*.

a. *Episcopus in ecclesia*. If "the bishop is in the church and the church is in the bishop," then achieving synodality in the local church and in the *communio ecclesiarum* means avoiding the episcopal ordination of many who hold positions in the Roman Curia and limiting the recourse to auxiliary bishops. Currently, more than half of the bishops in the world are bishops emeriti and titular bishops of local churches that no longer exist (in accord with canon 6 of Chalcedon).[73] Such a situation weakens the links between collegiality, service to a local church, and church synodality. Second, Cyprian's dictum suggests the synodal form of discernment that is needed today: the appointment of bishops[74] should involve the faithful, the priests, and the deacons of the local church. They are the ones who are best able to describe the local church's pastoral needs and provide a sort of "identikit" of the kind of bishop most appropriate, possibly also indicating names and motivations in a confidential context that is respectful of persons. The Council, in *Christus Dominus* 20, removed the appointment of bishops from the interference of political power, but it did not rethink the appointment of bishops in ways that would reflect the Council's more advanced ecclesiology.[75] The Council recognized the sacramentality and collegiality of the episcopate, thus changing its relationship with the Roman primacy, and it also enhanced the status of the local church, the primary subject of ecclesial life, stressing the co-responsibility of laity and clergy for the mission of the church. Despite the requests of many Fathers before and during the Council, *Christus Dominus* does not mention the possible involvement of the different ecclesial components in choosing candidates for the episcopate, as had happened in the early centuries when the election was *per clerum et populum*, nor does it indicate criteria for the selection of bishops (personal qualities, ecclesial experience, pastoral skills, studies, and so forth). The procedures for appointing bishops, which have changed several times in the course of history, are important not only for their pastoral implications and repercussions, but above all for their theological understanding of the figure of the bishop. Today, the central role in selection is played by the nuncios, with zero involvement of the local church; the system is highly centralized, lacking in transparency, and subject to ecclesiastical influences. It is far removed from the norms of the early church, which stated, "Let no bishop be imposed on the people whom the people reject" (Celestine I) and "The one who should preside over all must be elected by all" (Leo the Great).[76]

b. *Episcopus pater populi.* This expression leads us to consideration of how the bishop can and should exercise leadership in the local church.[77] Many modern dioceses are large in population and geographical extent and so require complex management structures that leave little room for close relations between the bishop and the laity; some bishops do not even have frequent and cordial relations with their priests and deacons. The universalistic vision of church that still prevails leads members to expect that the center, the Petrine Magisterium, will issue instructions for the whole church, without adequate concern for the inculturation of the faith in the local churches. Some bishops also seem reluctant to honor the pope's requests that they exercise greater autonomy from Rome in undertaking local initiatives.

The leadership by the bishops today appears weak in many ways: they have difficulty taking on a public role and motivating people to change; they react very slowly to a rapidly changing cultural world; they have difficulty finding the correct compromise (or balance) between implementing necessary changes and respecting existing institutions, between providing the institution with continuity and urging and guiding the people on the path of reform. Often the bishops appear isolated and remote in their pastoral ministry; in some parts of the world, they are burdened with endless bureaucratic and administrative tasks, while in other parts they suffer from a shortage of clergy, limited economic means, and social contexts that make diocesan management extremely difficult. The valuable indications that Vatican II gives on the exercise of the *munus regendi ac pascendi* in *Lumen Gentium* 27 and *Christus Dominus* 16[78] should be rethought from a synodal perspective, and recourse should be had to the metaphors of the family and the pastor. These metaphors suggest a specific style and function of the "one" with respect to the "all" and the collective—the church as family and as flock.

The challenge is to conceive of the church as a "cooperative system" that is ministerial in nature and asymmetrical in the relations between laity and ordained ministers. Such a system with a multiplicity of subjects is able to distinguish between the different powers and to create synodal structures and discernment practices that make clear the specific roles of the "one," the "some," and the "all." The *episkopé* can never be thought of as "absolutist" or "autarchic": by its very nature he is related to a multiplicity of subjects and ministerial figures. The bishop as subject has a unique responsibility and power in the "cooperative church system": he is responsible for the distribution of ministries and the church's overall organization, he guarantees the maturation of the *sensus fides ecclesiae* (the *munus docendi* of the bishops is related to the *con/sensus fidelium*, cf. DV 8), and he safeguards the catholicity of the *forma ecclesiae*, thus attesting to the specific identity of the local church over which he presides within the *communio ecclesiarum*. The bishop must never act in isolation from the other ecclesial subjects; rather, his leadership must be transformative and cooperative, for he is called to promote a collective process with the faithful that leads to maturation in the faith and permanent reform. As Cyprian, bishop of Carthage, declared: *nihil sine consilio vestro* (of you priests and deacons) *et sine consensu plebis.*[79]

Priests and Deacons

The document of the International Theological Commission on synodality is very restrained in what it says about the contribution of the other ordained ministers: priests and deacons are mentioned together in the discussion of the forms of exercising synodality in antiquity and in the Protestant reform (25, 32, 36); priests are said to be collaborators of the bishop and are thus identified with the "some" in the "one-some-all" triad (64, 60); and mention is made of the contribution of the Presbyteral Council (81), with a reference to *Presbyterorum Ordinis* 7, in which Pope Francis recalls the contribution that deacons and priests, cited jointly, make to the synodal assemblies. The specific contribution made by each of the two orders for the life of the local church is not indicated in either document, nor is it made explicit in the discussion of synodality at the parish level. But promotion of a synodal church clearly cannot be separated from a reconsideration of these ministerial figures and a reconfiguration of the ecclesial relationships in which they are protagonists.

As we have seen, Vatican II charted a profound theological renewal,[80] and it rethought the specific nature of the priesthood in relation to the bishop. In doing so, it reinterpreted the christological matrix that insisted on the sacred power and character of priests, and it overruled the logic that saw the priest as a mediator between God and the people, as an *alter Christus*. Such a view had been codified by the Council of Trent and nourished in spiritual formation by the French School and by certain pontifical documents up to the time of Pius XII. After centuries of oblivion, the diaconate was reinstituted by the Council as an autonomous and permanent order (LG 29; AG 16), and it was given specific tasks and functions in the *diakonia* of liturgy, Gospel, and charity. This theological interpretation has not always been actively and gladly accepted: instead, traditionalist interpretations of the priesthood are widespread, reproducing post-Tridentine mental and pastoral patterns and hindering a correct understanding of the priestly ministry of the people of God. To borrow the felicitous expression of A. Borras, the diaconate has been "betrayed by its novelty."[81] It has given rise to different types of ministers (Levite deacon, shepherd, Samaritan, prophet, and others) in a constant, unsettled oscillation between those who prefer service at the altar and those who emphasize the service of charity or catechesis. Meanwhile, the deacon remains unknown to most of the faithful.

Bearing in mind the various dynamics of the exercise of synodality and at the same time trying to grasp with clarity the source of postconciliar resistance, we can indicate some settled points on the membership of priests and deacons as well as some challenges that must be urgently addressed if the synodal processes are to avoid obstruction.

Two Complementary Ministries

The first indication comes from thinking conjointly about the subjectivity and the specific contributions of priests and deacons.[82] Vatican II does something of this nature by presenting a sort of diptych in *Lumen Gentium* 28–29 (the first drafts of *De Ecclesia* had only one paragraph, no. 15). Much can be learned also from the ritual action of the two orders in the eucharistic celebration, but it is not possible to elaborate a complete theology of the priesthood and then use it to shed light on the diaconate. It is necessary to overcome the "linear-vertical" hierarchical vision with its so-called scissors interpretation, by which the bishop is the head while the priest and the deacon are his two "arms." Instead, we must think of the relations among ordained ministers in terms of a "triangular system": the priests and deacons have their primary relation with the bishop but are also in relation to each other. On the one hand, in a synodal church, priests (those ordained *ad sacerdotium*) safeguard the apostolicity of the faith by guaranteeing the constitutive correlation between the gospel, the faith of Christians, and sacramental life; they serve as presidents of the community and of the Eucharist "*in persona Christi [capitis]*,"[83] as understood by the theology of the second millennium. The priest makes it clear that the professed faith is nourished and renewed through the sacraments, especially the Eucharist, so that it is lived out in daily life and nourishes the baptismal priesthood. Deacons,[84] on the other hand, have received the imposition of hands "*non ad sacerdotium sed ad ministerium*" (ordained nonpriestly ministry); they are responsible for safeguarding the apostolicity of the faith by guaranteeing the constitutive correlation between the gospel, the faith of Christians, and life in love.[85] They make it clear to all that a professed faith that fails to manifest itself as charity, especially toward those experiencing need and living in situations of poverty, is useless and contradictory because it denies its christological and trinitarian roots.

In the synodal dynamics of the church, the priests lead in the service of the "one" in the community or parish entrusted to them. They motivate discernment, understanding of the faith, and pastoral cooperation in communion with the bishop, and they give public voice to the contribution that comes from their communities. The deacons, for their part, offer a particular manner of reading the signs of the times and the characteristics and needs of their region. They face up to the demanding challenges of practicing prophetic justice and service in the world, especially for the poorest. Deacons manifest the evangelical ways of kenotic leadership;[86] theirs is a ministry exercised by accompanying the least and the last and by rejecting the logic of privilege and honor so as to be at the service of the communal journey of all. In a special way, the deacons are the first "eyes and ears of the bishop," the ones who know the local situation well and can identify the pastoral needs of our time. Accordingly, in synodal contexts— pastoral councils, assemblies, diocesan and episcopal synods— deacons contribute to communal discernment according to the criteria indicated in *Lumen Gentium* 8 (on being a poor church and a church of the poor) with their truly unique and irreplaceable word. The church's commitment to expanding the permanent diaconate of both celibate and married men, especially in those parts of the world in which the number of deacons is still limited, is a real contribution to a synodal church. The church is "unbalanced" when the ministerial figure of the deacon is missing. The diaconate also prevents any undue reduction of ordained ministry to the "priesthood" and so fosters more self-awareness in priests at the parish and diocesan levels.

The Challenge of Synodality for Priests and Deacons

Besides committing to the spread of the diaconate, there are two other ways in which the church can mature in synodality, thanks again to a new understanding of the ministers. When it envisioned the exercise of ministry and the ideal formation, the Gregorian-Tridentine vision insisted on the figure of the "individual" minister who is placed at the head of the community entrusted to him. The seminary, an "ingenious" invention of Trent, was designed to train priests for liturgical worship and *cura animarum*; their tasks included teaching well-defined doctrine and directing standardized pastoral activities, but promoting community processes of transformation was not part of their job description. In an almost totally male environment, the seminary[87] trains celibate men who will live alone, in circumstances quite different from those of the rest of the faithful. Thus, priests are not well prepared to face the challenges of pastoral life in today's parish. The seminary simply does not prepare them for the arduous task of being cultivators of community life, weavers of fraternal relationship, promoters of a widespread lay ministry that goes beyond the customary practices, creators of events that foster a sense of "we," and presiders at liturgical assemblies in which everyone can take an active part. At present, the formation of future priests takes place in ways and in contexts that are for the most part quite different from those that characterize the preparation of candidates for the diaconate and of laypeople for full-time pastoral work. The seminary offers little in the way of the pedagogical, psychological, and pastoral skills that are needed for guiding the community through the exercise of cooperative leadership and planning.

Synodality is not feasible without thorough reform of the initial and ongoing formation processes of those who are committed to full-time service of the community, whether they are priests, deacons, laity, religious, or (why not?) bishops. They should receive formation together as much as possible so that they will have a better understanding of the identity of each, their different charisms and ministries, and their relation to one another. Close interaction of this sort will make them aware that they are all engaged in a single mission that requires multiple paths and diverse contributions from both laypeople and ordained ministers. Formation proposals should also be devised that will help bishops guide the synodal pathways of the portion of the people of God entrusted to them (CD 11). As the ones primarily responsible for the community, bishops should lead not only by the power and authority linked to their position but by the example of their lives, by dialogue and persuasion, and by a thorough knowledge of the social and cultural context.[88] Synodal maturation also comes about as priests and deacons recognize themselves as part of a "collective body." Vatican II encouraged greater cooperation and sharing of the pastoral burden between bishop and priests, and it urged that the *presbyterium* be seen not as the sum of individuals but as a collective subject.[89] The instructions given in *Lumen Gentium* 28 and *Presbyterorum Ordinis* 7–8, 28 first found expression in presbyteral councils, in the appeal to priestly fraternity, and in the proposal of a common life among priests, but both theological reflection on this subject and actual practice still seem immature. Likewise, little thought has been given to deacons in this regard.

Ministers among God's People, with Others

A second, more radical challenge would allow a reconfiguration of ministries that truly expresses the synodal *mens* and provides a transformative means for making synodality effective on the symbolic and functional levels: we need to stop thinking of the individual ministerial figures in their "splendid isolation" but rather see them constitutively in relations of communion and pastoral cooperation. In redesigning the varied ministries of all the baptized in a synodal perspective, we should think of entrusting community leadership not to individual ordained ministers, but to pastoral teams[90] made up of laypeople, married or not, and ordained ministers: priests and deacons, including women deacons. Such a perspective will make it possible to situate ordained ministry—the priest's presiding service and the deacon's complementary ministry—within the framework of community life. The resulting coordination of ministerial responsibilities will help avoid clericalizing or sacralizing outcomes in the conception of the ministry and dangerous reductions of the power of the one before and over all.

Cooperative forms of governance will favor the acquisition and maturation of a spirituality of communion, and a shared leadership that is rich in charisms and experiences will motivate everyone to cooperate effectively in the one mission.[91] Clearly, the path of reform toward a synodal, participatory, service-oriented church[92] requires a different model for the understanding and exercise of ministries, ordained or not. Such a model does not contradict, either symbolically or operationally, the synodal instances we have mentioned. This change will emerge from combining theological reflection on existing innovative practices with the creative ability to promote new experiences that are able to anticipate the future. It is not a question either of claiming roles in the ecclesial body or of redistributing power so as to give space to those who have been neglected until now. Rather, the aim is to promote a dynamic of ecclesial life that measures up to the church's messianic mission in today's world, sixty years after Vatican II. Much depends on the ways in which ministry is exercised, on the style and dynamics of the service that is offered, and on the denunciation and elimination of any clerical logic that fragments the ecclesial body or prevents its maturation.

4

A Church of Co-responsibility

"A synodal Church is a Church of participation and co-responsibility. In exercising synodality she is called to give expression to the participation of all, according to each one's calling, with the authority conferred by Christ on the College of Bishops headed by the Pope."[1] In this passage, the document of the International Theological Commission on synodality summarizes the twofold dynamic of community participation and co-responsibility in the difference of charisms and ministries. The fundamentals of community participation were presented in paragraph 55, which reasserts the ecclesiological vision of Vatican II by giving priority to a strong pneumatological interpretation of ecclesial membership and ministries over the more traditional christological perspective:

> Synodality means that the whole Church is a subject and that everyone in the Church is a subject. The faithful are σύνοδοι, companions on the journey. They are

called to play an active role inasmuch as they share in the one priesthood of Christ and are meant to receive the various charisms given by the Holy Spirit in view of the common good. Synodal life reveals a Church consisting of free and different subjects, united in communion, which is dynamically shown to be a single communitarian subject built on Christ, the cornerstone, and on the Apostles, who are like pillars, built like so many living stones into "a spiritual house" (cf. 1 Peter 2:5), "a dwelling-place of God in the Spirit" (Ephesians 2:22).

Co-responsibility was referred to in the ITC's reflection on the dynamics of the Jerusalem assembly according to Acts 15: "So all are equally responsible for the life and mission of the community, and all are called to work in accordance with the law of mutual solidarity in respect of their specific ministries and charisms, inasmuch as every one of them finds his or her energy in the one Lord (cf. 1 Corinthians 15:45)."[2]

As stated in 1 Peter 2:5, the church is called to co-construct itself as a "house of the Spirit" for proclaiming and understanding the gospel (see LG 12; DV 8) and for the service of all. The ecclesiological vision of Vatican II is rooted in the principle of proclamation that creates church, not in the principle of delegated authority that serves as the basis of the corporate, hierarchical ecclesiology of the whole second millennium. The equal dignity and the common responsibility of all the baptized is reaffirmed with great clarity in LG 31, and awareness of this should support the pathways leading to an "all-ministerial church" that is committed to a single mission in a multiplicity of ways, tasks, services, and ministries (AA 2).

The questions concerning the related themes of the foundation and recognition of the subjectivity of all, the relational and participatory forms, and the development of ministry in the church must be faced with courage and creativity to promote ecclesial synodality, and they must be interwoven with the contributions of systematic theology, reflections on actual pastoral practices, and canon law. An examination, even a superficial one, of the reception of Vatican II in Latin America, Africa, and Europe shows that certain transformative dynamics are working in this direction.[3] There is a variety of ministries that go beyond the subjectivity of the clergy; many diverse and valuable contributions are coming from the laity, who offer new languages and skills that enrich the life of the church. With the emergence of the "gender question" in the church, women are achieving greater self-awareness and are assuming increasingly significant public ecclesial responsibilities. With the decrease in the number of women religious, changes have taken place in women's religious life. Meanwhile, the decrease in the number of priests and the increase in their average age has brought on a crisis of the "clerical system" of formation and the exercise of the ministry, a crisis made apparent by the denunciation of sexual, economic, and financial abuses, as well as abuses of conscience. Finally, there has been an increase in the number of deacons, especially married ones, and of full-time lay pastoral workers. These phenomena, which to varying degrees and in different forms characterize local churches around the world, are at the heart of the current synodal debates. This successful reception of the Council's requests is also impelling changes in theology (especially the theology of orders, of priesthood, and of ministry) and in renewed ministerial practices and structures. Of course, there is resistance, such as the glass ceiling affecting women and the laity more generally, the persistence of a Tridentine *mens* ("mind") and model of church, and the return of a sacralized logic that stresses clerical privilege and a "caste" system. All these are difficult to overcome, but building a church of believers who recognize themselves as co-responsible members and act correspondingly requires us to denounce and thoroughly expunge clericalism, an evil that has ancient roots and produces fruits that poison ecclesial relations.

CLERICALISM

In sections 73 and 104 of the synodality document of the International Theological Commission, two brief references are made to the clerical mentality as an obstacle to the realization of synodality. Pope Francis has made the term *clericalism*[4] a leitmotif of his teaching, so much so that on more than sixty occasions he has described it with harsh words, speaking of it as a "disease" (2014), an "evil," a "plague," a "sin," and a "very great disease" (2016–2017). He called clericalism a "plague" and a "perversion of the church" eleven times between 2018 and 2020 and considered it "one of the greatest deformations."[5] He described clericalism as "a temptation" that affects both clerics and laity (2013), though in different ways.

The clergy affected by clericalism devalue baptismal grace, fail to recognize and to value the contribution of the laity, and betray their missionary vocation. For their part, the clericalized laity are submissive before priests, or they demand roles that are not theirs, assuming a sacralized logic. There is, says the pope, "a kind of active clericalism, desired and nurtured by the clergy, and also a passive clericalism, accepted and suffered by the laity."[6] Clericalism is a very serious evil for the church because it has a serious misunderstanding at its core: it falsifies the identity of *one's own* subjectivity, either as a priest or as a layperson, and it falsifies the identity of *other* ecclesial subjects. Moreover, it injects a noxious injustice into ecclesial relationships, and it misrepresents the nature of power and authority. The heart of clericalism, both for priests and for laity, lies in its failure to overcome a pyramidal vision of the church and a hierarchical, sacralized vision of ordained ministry. Clericalism fails to take on board the theology of the people and the renewed understanding of the ministry of bishops, priests, and deacons.

As Pope Francis reminds us, ordained clergy who think of their ministry as a power to be exercised rather than as a free and generous service to be offered to others are guilty of a "caricature and perversion of ministry"; they are characterized by self-referentiality, "authoritarianism," and "arrogance and tyranny." Clericalism leads ministers on a "personal quest to occupy, monopolize, and control spaces by minimizing and nullifying the anointing of the people of God"; it motivates clergy to pursue "functional, paternalistic, possessive, and even manipulative ties" with others.

Clericalism therefore affects primarily the self-awareness of the clergy and only secondarily that of the laity. It is a serious pathology that cannot be reduced simply to the temptations or errors of individuals who are not sufficiently formed or mature. As the Final Report of the Royal Commission in Australia denounces,[7] the ecclesial system—in its formation and in its structuring of internal relations—is deeply marked by a clerical culture whose manifestations include "an authoritarian style of ministerial leadership, a rigidly hierarchical cosmovision, and a virtual identification of the holiness and grace of the church with the clerical state." This culture is generated and maintained by appealing to a vision of church and ministry that justifies the "special consecration" of some with respect to the rest of the faithful, and it is intensified through pastoral practices—including liturgies, symbols, ceremonies, language, idioms, styles of behavior, and expectations—that glorify the clergy to the exclusion of others.

A Church of Co-responsibility

Such clericalism is not infrequently wedded to patriarchal and androcentric logics. Ordination produces a sense of belonging to a social body (the clergy) that provides identity, guarantees social recognition, identifies a functional role, and specifies a path of spirituality and holiness. Clericalism is nourished by an affirmation of self that avoids an authentic confrontation with the other (the laity) that can give clerics a sense of their limits and reduce their exaggerated sense of importance in the ecclesial network. Clericalism affirms the "one" who is "over all" or "before all," an attitude found in bishops and priests that is far removed from the ideal of ministry as being "one-with-all and one-for-all."

True synodal reform requires an inner conversion because only synodal, participatory experiences will help to deconstruct the clerical mentality. Overcoming clericalism implies "thinking differently" and discarding false or partially erroneous conceptions of ordained ministry; it requires interrupting sacralized practices that have nothing to do with the following of Jesus; and it means abandoning the "logic of the elite" and the pursuit of ecclesiastical careers. Finally, it means eliminating the culture of secrecy and all forms of clerical or caste-based corporatism. We must fearlessly question the image of priest that is taught in the seminary, where students learn a system of intra-ecclesial relations made up of symbols, languages, robes, and forms of life that highlight distinction (and separation) rather than humble service to and among the people of God. Titles taken on centuries ago—father, monsignor, reverend, excellency—express forms of social and ecclesial life that are far removed from those of the laity; such titles must be abandoned because they convey the idea of superiority and encourage an unconscious acceptance of anti-synodal logic.[8]

Men and women who cherish the dream of a synodal church must exercise constant vigilance in the face of any resurgence of clericalism; they should insist on paths of formation that jettison the "splendid isolation" sought by some clerics or that reinforce a mentality that emphasizes sacralized separation rather than unreserved involvement in the journey of the people of God.

PARTICIPATION

How can co-responsibility be promoted in the church? What conditions and places are required for community discernment and shared pastoral service?

Participation, in the twofold sense of "being part" and "taking part," requires, first, the promotion of paths of *"empowerment"*[9] so that all ecclesial members become aware of their power to act according to their proper roles and possibilities. The laity, for their part, should seek to remedy their lack of self-awareness and feelings of resignation by taking courses in biblical and theological formation or by attending workshops on the documents of Vatican II. Bishops or priests, however, should seek to overcome any vestiges of a "distorted self-awareness" that is often self-centered and fails to acknowledge its limits, or that does not understand its "relative nature" and recognize its identity within the synodal network of "one, some, and all."[10] In a synodal church, identities must be rethought in conjunction and in accord with a differentiation of functions, a differentiation understood precisely in relation to the one mission that is served by all but in different ways and with asymmetrical relationships of communication and decision-making.

For this reason, the second challenge is that of *"entitlement"*[11] in the literal sense: "to have a title for exercising a given function." This undoubtedly depends on the members, who not only affirm their right to participate but declare their capacity, competence, and aptitude to perform the related functions. But it also depends on the recognition that the members receive (or do not receive). In entitlement there is always a fundamental cognitive component, namely, the self-judgment of the specific members involved. While this is experienced on the affective and motivational level of action, it also involves the paths that give access to certain roles and organizational structures on the institutional level, as well as the social and operational expectations of all those who work in each organization.

Entitlement is a question of "role taking" by individual members and of "role making" by the social body and by the individuals capable of designating new "ministerial figures" that will then be extended to all. Whether the necessary conditions— innate and acquired—for access to new roles are in fact created is determined, on the one hand, by the ecclesial body as a whole and, on the other, by all the subjects involved who develop an authentic judgment of themselves in comparison with others, taking into account not only the norms in force at the time but also the feasibility of implementing behaviors and practices that are different from those received from the past.

The reform of ministry in the church for the various ecclesial actors, as we have indicated, requires serious work in four areas at the same time: (1) as much as possible, initial and ongoing formation should be imparted jointly for laypeople and ordained ministers, giving priority to times and places that are acceptable and sustainable for the laity; (2) team work should be the norm, involving moments of shared planning, implementation, and verification in which the different charisms and ministries offer their respective contributions; (3) a dynamics of multidirectional communication and participation should allow everyone to be both "listener and transmitter" in the communications network; (4) the structures of the extensive organizational culture, with its differentiated roles, should be revised so that existing gaps and exclusion procedures are eliminated, unjustified stereotypes are rejected, and new ministerial figures are creatively promoted in response to the changing needs of the church and society.

From the point of view of praxis, the promotion of a synodal church requires a continuous and meticulous discernment of charisms.[12] It is not just a matter of seeking pastoral workers for activities decided in advance by "some" (parish priest, pastoral council), but of entering into contact with every adult baptized person so that, through dialogue, they can fully grasp what they are able to offer the community, by gift of the Spirit. Such an approach will generate new forms of service and new activities, thus overcoming the restriction of pastoral action to "the handful of usual collaborators."

> The laity must grow in their ability to interpret the faith and wisely support the journey of the community as a whole. Besides generously attending to their customary ministries, lay people should also take on new ones, giving life to innovative forms of education in the faith and pastoral care, always in the logic of ecclesial communion.[13]

REDESIGNING RELATIONSHIPS, AUTHORITY ROLES, AND THE EXERCISE OF POWER

With more and more laypeople assuming pastoral responsibilities that for centuries have been the exclusive domain of male clerics, we see revealed the implicit, tacitly accepted rules underlying the organizational culture that is widespread in the church. The active presence of the laity is provoking the necessary dislocation of the ordained ministers, who are forced to rethink their own identities in relation to the laity, thus changing the fabric of intra-ecclesial relations with new interactions. The identities of both laity and ordained ministers undergo a process of transformation, or rather a process of mutual repositioning (vis-à-vis the community) and of mutual social construction (including in terms of gender): "Subjects are constituted by and through a symbolic system that gives them a position even beyond the members' full awareness."[14]

What Power?

Becoming a synodal church requires a rethinking of the forms of the exercise of power[15] and especially the nature of "the authority of Pastors, [which] is a specific gift of the Spirit of Christ the Head for the upbuilding of the entire Body, not a delegated and representative function of the people."[16] Speaking about the synodal church begins with the "power of" word in the church, without focusing only on the one's "power over" all; it involves enhancing every form of "power with."[17] The ideal horizon of a cooperative form of governance does not exclude completely the asymmetry linked to the specific ministry of the ordained, who safeguard the apostolicity of the faith in service to the institutionalized "ecclesial We," but it does not absolutize the "power of one"; instead, it recognizes and promotes the multiplicity of powers in the church and seeks to overcome hierarchical logic. As Ephesians 4:7–16 clearly reminds us, the ecclesial body grows in faith through the contributions that all Christians ("the saints") make in the work of *diakonia* (*ergon tes diakonias*), the service to which everyone should dedicate themselves with the help of those who exercise pastoral ministry.

In the church, everyone is called to serve and to contribute to the growth and maturation of the community; certain ministries of the word are oriented toward the existence and subsistence of the church as the "church of Jesus" based on the apostolic faith. Ordained ministries are necessary and constitutive; they are oriented to pursuing the good of the community, preserving its identity, and guaranteeing its dynamic growth in Christ. However, they should not think of themselves as substituting for the "all," whose singular contribution, the fruit of the Spirit's capacious and diversifying creativity, they must recognize, promote, value, and coordinate for the common work. Unity and diversity constitute the two fundamental registers of a synodal church and explain its dynamism.[18]

What Leadership?

"The question of Christian ministry remains a burning issue. The life of the church depends on it. The hope of renewal … remains alive, sustained by the faith that animates Christians in the power of the Holy Spirit."[19] For the synodal church to become a reality, it is necessary to define the form of leadership best suited to the common path.[20] The time is long past both for positional leaders, those who operate on the basis of the role received, and for transactional leaders, those who operate by the logic of incentives and negotiations. Both types simply manage what already exists or else implement slow, incremental changes; neither type can foster a collective identity or contribute to a "common reason" for strengthening ecclesial relationships. The journey of the people of God and the enactment of synodal forms can be achieved only by "transformational leadership"[21] that is capable of inspiring the desired changes, motivating people to work for the common good, mobilizing energy to move from individual to collective interests, actively involving "intermediate bodies," and constantly calling everyone, by an exemplary life and meaningful words, to the final objective. The church today needs leadership, from both ordained ministers and full-time lay pastoral agents; it must be leadership nourished by a synodal style and so committed to creating synodal forms and appropriate structures in the management of power. We cannot rely solely on the hard power that is linked to authority roles in the ecclesiastical structure that have hitherto enjoyed high social recognition and have constituted the Catholic Church's effective bureaucratic organization. A truly transformational, cooperative leadership must know how to balance this first aspect of the "power of role" with both soft power—emotional intelligence, empathy, the ability to discern the needs of individuals, verbal and symbolic communication skills, and so on, and smart power—the ability to adapt to the contexts, perceive appropriate times, and take advantage of current trends adapting current strategies and the rhythm of joint action.[22]

Ordained ministers, especially bishops, are not currently trained to manage complex processes[23] that are implemented through phases and with contributions from intermediate agents who act on their own initiative (and not simply as transmitters of what is defined by their hierarchical superiors) with a view to transforming the people. This shortcoming has a substantial impact on the possibility and timing of synodal reform, especially when it comes to treating complex theological issues and their pastoral implications. Elderly pastoral leaders (the Catholic Church appears at times to be a gerontocracy) are often reluctant to change; they prefer to leave the task of carrying out a profound transformation to those who will come later. At this time, pastoral immobility is truly dangerous.

CO-RESPONSIBLE FOR THE FUTURE

As early as the 1990s, Bernard Sesboüé wrote about the new forms of ministry:

> Whether we like it or not, the Catholic Church is faced with important decisions. Today, these decisions are caught in a bind between patience and urgency. Patience and serenity are necessary: it would be a waste of time to make these decisions in a climate of emotional pressure, without having carefully considered what is at stake for the future of the church. It is a question of thinking about the time required for transition and experimentation, as well as for the evolution of outlooks...but an excess of prudence risks being the worst of imprudence. An absence of decisions risks being the worst of decisions.[24]

Coming together for meetings and synodal processes represents a school of communion that provides a precious space for the mutual recognition of identity. At the same time, it allows people to grasp more immediately the urgency of change and the challenges ahead. In this way they share pastoral responsibility in the open process of building the church, for which all the baptized are indeed responsible. Etymologically, "responsibility" designates the capacity to respond to the needs, problems, appeals, and challenges that come from reality; it requires measuring the effect of the response not only on the present, but also on the promised or desired future. As Dietrich Bonhoeffer stated, responsibility is measured on wholeness and on hope. Responsibility is "the totality and the unity of the response to reality given to us in Christ, as opposed to the partial responses we might give on the basis, for

example, of considerations of expediency or certain principles."
Moreover, "for the responsible person the ultimate question is
not: how heroically am I performing in this matter? but rather:
how will the coming generation be able to continue to live?"[25]

A synodal church is a church that assumes responsibility
for the future, knowing that only the contributions of all in word
and action can open appropriate paths to the change we desire.
Opting for synodality means deepening spiritual and theological
principles so that all the baptized accept them and make them
their own, but it also entails real changes in the form of relationships so that they may become dialogical and inclusive. Synodality likewise demands a decisive commitment on the level of
structures, which do not change automatically due to new ways
of thinking or the enthusiasm that comes from new relational
dynamics.

5

The Reform of Structures

THE STRUCTURES

The church is a "restless body" (S. Xeres).[1] The "ecclesial We," the church—both the members who compose it and its institutional figure—is marked by continuous change, which is sometimes very slow, almost imperceptibly, and at other times faster and more clearly identifiable. In the past, it has also been marked by some major reforms, especially the Gregorian and Tridentine.[2] Alongside the constant incremental evolution of dynamic change, some rare processes of *reform* can be recognized. This term, as its etymology shows, refers to the complex dynamics by which an organization or institution gives itself "a new form," thus configuring itself differently.[3] The process of renewal that takes place touches the very "figure" of the church, its overall historical "configuration," and not simply some of its dimensions, activities, or practices. Church reform has to do with a global refoundational renewal, a process that affects the subject "church" in all its aspects, subjects, and dynamics: it affects the empirically observable figure and seeks reinterpretation of the categories of self-definition.[4] The reference paradigm changes, and the ecclesial figure changes. The transformation is structural and not simply an adaptation or incremental evolution. While micro changes are routine even for the church (this is the natural state of any organization, argues March), reforms are intentional: "reforms differ from change in that they involve explicit descriptions of the state that is desired and striven for."[5]

Consciousness, Form, and Synodal Processes

Every reform takes place when people act consciously and deliberately on the three different coexisting and correlated levels of the life of the organization in question, and their action on the three levels will be effective and significant to the extent that it is organic and systematic. First, the church's self-awareness must be rethought and reshaped; second, the forms of relationship and collective behavior must be remodeled; and third, institutionalized structures must be reorganized regarding both their functionality and their symbolic implications.[6] Reform takes place simultaneously on these interrelated levels; it must be motivated and experienced on all these planes, and their interconnections must be understood. A changed understanding of the collective consciousness requires not only a new relational experience but also new communicative and participative structures. However, for these transformations to be organized and promoted, they need to be supported by a certain "ecclesiological vision" with new images, categories, and languages. The transformations affect not only rites and symbols but also norms of behavior, procedures, structures, and relationships. Deconstruction begins on a symbolic level but then is combined with a progressive redefinition and reshaping of educational dynamics, participatory communicative structures, and inclusive decision-making spaces.

After an initial phase, in which there is usually enthusiasm but also growing resistance, it is necessary to identify the resources available to accompany the long processes of transformation: every reform must be energized by motivation, solid understanding, and responses to problems that envision a desirable future. It is important to make the most of the spaces and opportunities that the Code of Canon Law and liturgical usages already allow. Real change in the logic of action and relationships within an institution, however, requires much time and a steady, careful process that progressively reshapes collective ideas and behavior. The rethinking of ecclesial structures is essential if the process of ecclesial reform is to be effective and meaningful.[7] The task is an arduous one, and it calls for creativity and courage in the deconstruction and the progressive delineation of innovative modes, contexts, procedures, and institutions.

The Local Churches

Our reflection will focus on the local church as a "*portio* of the people of God" gathered around the bishop in proclaiming the gospel and celebrating the Eucharist; it is where the church of Christ *vere inest et operatur* (*Christus Dominus* 11).[8] In the local church, all the basic dynamics for a synodal church are present. The reform of the entire church, the *corpus ecclesiarum*, cannot disregard this nuclear level of the "ecclesial We": the *Catholica* exists in and from the local churches (*in quibus et ex quibus*, according to the famous passage of *Lumen Gentium* 23). Reform from a synodal perspective touches both the figure of the diocesan church and the parishes, which are the "parts" of the diocese in which belonging and participation are experienced in a more immediate way, and in which many of the activities of proclamation, Christian formation, and sacramental life are carried out.

Various theological and pastoral reasons make reflection on this reality urgent. First, the Council's rethinking of the ministry of the bishop,[9] which recovered the sacramentality (LG 21) and the collegiality (LG 22–23) of the episcopate, was accompanied by the beginnings of an ecclesiological vision of the local churches that moved beyond the universalist Gregorian-Tridentine system ratified by Vatican I (see LG 26, 28; SC 41). These developments led to a new figure of the diocese, as becomes clear in the pastoral and juridical indications of the decree *Christus Dominus*.[10] Second, the parish model developed during the second millennium, whose fundamental elements were defined by the Council of Trent and were then developed in the following four centuries, appears inadequate for today's culture. The model does not correspond to the ecclesiology of Vatican II even though it is widespread throughout the world and deeply rooted in the mentality of the ordained ministers and many of the faithful.

The maturation of synodality as the church's *modus vivendi et operandi* cannot help but affect these two models of ecclesial life: not only the fundamental level of the local church but also the parish, which is close to everyone's experience but is derivative and transient in nature and not "necessary" regarding its form.

For each of these two levels, we will point out the institutions in which synodality, in fact, takes place and the changes that are needed today to become a "synodal church." Finally, regarding both levels, we will address the delicate issue of deliberation in the church, for transformative processes and the development of permanent synodal dynamics are possible only if we work for changes in the way decisions are made at all levels, from the parish to the diocese to the universal church.[11]

A SYNODAL DIOCESE

In his speech on the occasion of the fiftieth anniversary of the institution of the Synod of Bishops, Pope Francis indicated that the "first level for exercising synodality"[12] is the local church.[13] The document issued by the International Theological Commission, "Synodality in the Life and Mission of the Church," outlines an organic framework for implementing synodality in the local church, for it is there that a special manifestation of the church takes place insofar as all the components of the people of God participate in understanding the faith and in co-responsible pastoral action.[14]

During the Council, an understanding of the church as starting out from the local churches gradually matured and succeeded in overcoming the universalist vision that had characterized the ecclesial experience throughout the second millennium. E. Lanne suggests that the new understanding represents a "Copernican turning point,"[15] even if Vatican II did not develop a complete, organic treatment of the matter. The theme was not initially foreseen and was dealt with only indirectly, in relation to other topics such as the relationship of the church and the Eucharist (see SC 41; LG 26), episcopal collegiality (LG 23), and the theology of mission (AG 22). We find the most systematic and organic definition of the particular/local church in *Christus Dominus* 11, but there is no treatment of it in the context where one would expect it, the second chapter of *Lumen Gentium*. Most of the guidelines for transforming the pastoral life of the dioceses are to be found in the decree on the ministry and life of the bishops.

Sixty years after Vatican II, despite the incompleteness and unsystematic nature of the conciliar documents on the subject (evident in the terminological oscillation between local and particular), there has been a clear maturation of awareness on the ecclesiological level, and there have been significant pastoral transformations of the local churches, including dioceses, prelatures, and apostolic vicariates. Reflection on how a local church can be synodal is therefore the first strategic step for thinking about the reform of synodal structures, processes, procedures, and institutions. The words of Karl Rahner are still valid: "We can and must deepen our reflection on this 'local' ecclesiology; we can and must make it alive in ourselves. A huge amount of work awaits us in this field."[16] This process entails many changes, including the pastoral conversion of all, from the bishop to the lay faithful. The process requires new modes of formation and renewal of relationships. It should produce novel public signs of ecclesial presence, dynamic communications, and structures that facilitate participation, co-responsibility, and operational synergy that contribute to the "ecclesial We."[17]

Steps of Ordinary Synodality

Since synodality is a constitutive dimension of the church and so must become its *modus vivendi et operandi*,[18] it is evident that all aspects of pastoral life and all diocesan activities must be rethought from this perspective. In *Evangelii Gaudium*, the pope encouraged the faithful to undertake ordinary pastoral work from a missionary perspective (see EG 27), and this counsel also applies to synodality. Synodality is firstly a matter of rethinking the relationships, activities, and structures of the ordinary pastoral care in a diocese from a synodal perspective. They should reflect a synodal form of church and be a means for bringing about ever greater participation, co-responsibility, and cooperation, all the while allowing for the creation of new styles of relationship and ecclesial action that embody the primary instances of synodality—listening to all, letting all speak, synergy, community discernment, and so on.

Analysis of the Situation

A first essential step, therefore, is analyzing and diagnosing the ecclesial and pastoral situation so as to detect attitudes, habits, mentalities, procedures, and structures that, in effect, deny the synodal form, obstruct its most genuine expressions, or even try to negate it. At the same time, the analysis and diagnosis should seek out the resources, experiences, and structures in which synodality has already become a reality. The problems are manifold: the "synodal gaps" that insist on only certain subjects and contexts; the real barriers (mental and procedural) that deny full participation of speech and action to all; and the lack of good leadership in the conduct of collective processes. Other problems are the lack of transparency, information unduly reserved to a few, scant creativity in the forms of communication, little willingness to listen to the people about what concerns them most, and the widespread culture of secrecy. These are some of the things that render communication ineffective, making it deaf to the real speech of all and incapable of considering the laity as co-responsible partners. Such characteristics reveal an ecclesial culture that contradicts the demands of the gospel. The inadequacy of the formation of both ordained ministers and the laity, albeit in different fields, makes it difficult to assess the different experiences, expectations, and impulses for reform. Even when these factors are present, they are often not supported by a solid biblical and theological foundation or by a thorough understanding of human existence, culture, knowledge, and science. All these issues must be patiently investigated and have their declared or unconscious assumptions deconstructed; they must be decisively tackled with the extreme patience that is required by all processes of cultural transformation.

Second, action can already be taken on certain diocesan pastoral practices of the Latin churches that were precisely regulated by the Council of Trent and rethought in *Christus Dominus*, specifically, the pastoral visits of the bishop[19] and the pastoral letters.

In the first case, the bishop's real encounter with the people should ensure that there is sufficient time for listening and for free discussion with all members of the communities and with those who have fallen away. Such an encounter makes it possible to integrate the triad "one," "some" (pastoral workers, pastoral council), and "all" on the level of pastoral discernment, even in the largest parishes. The relinquishing during the pastoral visit of bureaucratic forms that have little to do with the practical experience of community life will help the formation of a synodal mentality on such occasions. Similarly, the bishop's response to the community, in the form of a letter or a document, must go beyond the vague language of general counsels and touch concretely on the community's specific problems. The pastoral visit of the bishop can also be a moment for evaluating the ways in which ordinary synodality is revealed in parishes, communities, and groups; it can be an occasion for creating moments and structures that allow for broader and fuller participation of the faithful.

The procedures of some dioceses for drafting the bishop's pastoral letter could well be adopted and adapted by others: one or two questions are proposed on which all the faithful and all the parishes, associations, and communities are asked to express their views. Theologians and other competent persons can offer resource material from biblical texts, tradition, or the human sciences. The faithful can discuss with the priests and deacons the questions proposed and debate the responses received. Finally, the letter is drafted by the bishop after he has accepted this input and dialogued with all the components of ecclesial life; in the letter he offers a few indications of what can be implemented by all for the common diocesan path, and he recommends that the actual implementation be evaluated after some time. In the same way, since every local church thrives and matures by "religiously listening to the Word of God," the bishop's *munus docendi* and *munus pascendi* can take the form of choosing a biblical book every year for study by the whole diocese. The Bible study would guide the synodal path of formation as the faithful meditate on the text personally and discuss it in small groups. Such a process of exegetical reading would help to form pastoral workers, young people, and others, and it would strengthen the biblical-theological maturity and the general formation of the whole diocesan community.

Communicating as Church

Third, given the constitutive correlation between "communicating" and "organizing relations" to come together as an "ecclesial We," the existing communicational dynamics must be reconfigured at all levels, both for sharing information and for maturing ideas, projects, and activities. New ecclesial members, such as young people, must be involved, and the flow of information must be conveyed in a multidirectional way. It is not enough to adopt the "top-down" or "diocesan center/parish periphery" models of today's predominant communicational patterns. Even when such models allow feedback, they maintain the customary vertical, unidirectional logic, which is totally inadequate.

A new "communications system" must be designed and promoted to include moments for coming together (as diocese, as zones, as deanery, and so forth); councils and groups that discuss specific topics; and research seminars involving experts. All these elements should act in a flexible manner; they are not necessarily permanent structures. Communication channels must be developed that make use of diverse languages and modes of expression for different groups of members. Other ways of organizing participation are needed that respond to local customs and present needs, but they should always guarantee networked, "horizontal" communication. We are increasingly aware that communication shapes the internal organization and shape of the church:[20] discursive practices play a primary role in the formation of individuals, in the definition of collective identity, and in concretely enabling joint action. In talking about synodality, we should shift from a static reading of the church as "institution" to a dynamic interpretation of the processes that keep it alive and develop its form and its mission—the "synodal institutionalization of the church."[21]

The church is continuously "reconfigured" by its members through interactions that are symbolically mediated and communicated.[22] Communication is not one element among many in an already formed institution; it is the vital framework of every institution. We need to decide what communicative dynamics we want to put in place as the most appropriate means for organizing a synodal church.[23] Dialogue, conversation, debate, information exchange, and communicative interaction—all have a constitutive force: they generate relationships, they shape organizations and institutions that last over time, and they create consensus and a spirit of responsible participation. Church reform comes about through the promotion of a culture of dialogue and the creation of multiple spaces for conversation that are staffed by well-trained facilitators. Dialogue is never simply reproductive: it is always generative because it brings about confrontation with the other. This is especially the case not only when it is oriented toward managing the parts of the system, but also when it acts as a medium for change in the system, combining techniques of dialogue that generate new ideas and strategic dialogue. That is why it is useful to draw on the contributions of organizational sociologists, communications experts, psychologists, and pedagogues.

The "synodal option" requires certain changes in structures. Many aspects of the church require serious rethinking: the diocesan curia,[24] pastoral offices and commissions, the organization of groups of parishes in a territory (vicariates, deaneries, pastoral areas), the coordination of the activities of lay associations and movements, financial management, and the active involvement of consultors, episcopal councils, and cathedral chapters.[25]

Such rethinking will make it possible to practice the ongoing community discernment described by the bishops in the 1995 Conference of the Italian Church:

> Community discernment becomes a school of Christian life, a way to develop mutual love, co-responsibility, and integration in the world, starting with one's own territory. It builds up the church as a community of brothers and sisters, all of equal dignity but with different gifts and tasks, and it shapes the figure of a church, which, without straying into democratic and sociological issues, will be credible in today's democratic society. This practice should be spread at the level of groups, educational communities, religious families, parishes, pastoral areas, dioceses, and even at wider levels. Those responsible for Christian communities should deepen their understanding of community discernment and the ways in which they can promote it as authoritative spiritual and pastoral guides, wise educators, and effective communicators.[26]

Communal discernment is also envisaged in the Final Document of the Synod for Amazonia:

> To walk together, the Church today needs to be converted to the synodal experience. It is necessary to strengthen a culture of dialogue, mutual listening, spiritual discernment, consensus, and communion in order to find spaces and ways to reach shared decisions and respond to pastoral challenges. In this way, co-responsibility in the life of the Church will be promoted in a spirit of service. ....The Church in Amazonia is called to exercise discernment, which is at the heart of synodal processes and events. It is a matter of determining the path to be followed in the service of God's plan through theological interpretation of the signs of the times, under the guidance of the Holy Spirit, and then walking that path as a Church. Community discernment makes it possible to discover how God is calling us in any given historical situation. This Assembly is a moment of grace for exercising mutual listening, sincere dialogue, and community discernment for the common good of the People of God in the Amazon Region.[27]

Two other special moments of synodality deserve careful reflection: first, the diocesan synod, which is an *extraordinary* event in the life of the diocese, constitutes one of the most significant moments of epiphany for the local church; and second, the pastoral and presbyteral councils, which are *ordinary* instruments of community discernment and coordination of diocesan life, can become contexts for the promotion of authentic synodality if the work and the dialogue are conducted in a way that is effective and open to learning from all.

The Diocesan Synod

The document of the International Theological Commission presents the implementation of synodality in the local church starting precisely from the diocesan synod, which it calls the "highest of all diocesan structures of participation," "an act of episcopal governance, and an event of communion." The document describes in quick succession how the different ecclesial components contribute to the synodal event.[28] The diocesan synod, even if it is not explicitly mentioned in the conciliar documents, reveals the face of the church as the people of God of Vatican II. The ITC document outlines what roles are proper to the bishop and other components of the local church and how they relate directly to the theology of the ordained ministry and the laity as spelled out in *Lumen Gentium* and *Christus Dominus*, a theology situated in the postconciliar reception process that has seen significant development both in practice and in theological and magisterial elaboration.[29]

In 2011, A. Join-Lambert estimated that about 25 percent of dioceses had celebrated or were in the process of celebrating a diocesan synod.[30] This institution was referred to in the two directories for the ministry of bishops, *Ecclesiae Imago* (1973) and *Apostolorum Successores* (1994).[31] In 1997, an instruction on diocesan synods was published jointly by the Congregation for Bishops and the Congregation for the Evangelization of Peoples.[32] The diocesan synod is an ancient institution[33] that has developed in close correlation with the various phases of church reform, such as in the Carolingian era, after Lateran IV, and after the Council of Trent. The novelty made possible by Vatican II becomes clear if we compare the statements in the 1917 Pio-Benedictine Code (canons 356–62) with those in the 1983 Code of Canon Law (canons 460–68) regarding its participants, purpose, and periodicity.[34]

Canon 460 reads,

> The diocesan synod is an assembly of selected priests and other members of Christ's faithful of a particular Church which, for the good of the whole diocesan community, assists the diocesan Bishop in accordance with the following canons.

The synod is no longer the prerogative of the clergy alone, as had been the case from the twelfth century on; the laity are now also called upon to be active protagonists[35] of this event whose purpose is to assist the bishop and serve "the good of the whole diocesan community." Canon 6 of Lateran IV established an annual frequency, and this was reaffirmed by Trent (Session XXIV *de reformatione*). The frequency was changed to every three years by Vatican I and to every ten years in the Code of 1917. The 1983 Code does not define the periodicity but leaves the convocation to pastoral discernment concerning the local church's needs and the specific issues to be discussed. The diocesan synod does not have only a legislative purpose, nor does it simply apply to the local context the guidelines previously codified for the universal church. Rather, it envisages a more broadly "pastoral" perspective whose purpose is to shape the specific face of the "local" church. *Ecclesiae Imago* (163) indicates five functions of the diocesan synod: adapting universal laws to the particular church; indicating methods of apostolic work; overcoming difficulties in the apostolate and governance; stimulating pastoral initiatives; and correcting any errors in faith and customs.[36]

Eugene Duffy[37] refers to several other aspects: kerygmatic work; inculturation of the faith and the church in the specific social and cultural context; and planning of pastoral action around precisely determined themes, especially those that aid the overall reception of Vatican II in the postconciliar season. The synod provides a unique opportunity for maturing the figure of the church in all its originality, always keeping in mind the local culture and history, which always have traits of uniqueness and so can make a singular contribution to the *corpus ecclesiarum*.

When proposing a synodal conversion aimed at church structures, this reference to the diocesan synod seems almost obvious, but pursuing such an objective requires addressing certain unresolved questions that have come to light in the widespread synodal practice. Numerous studies on this topic have been done by theologians and canonists.[38] The positive outcome of a diocesan synod depends firstly on the choice of the topic to be discussed.[39] If the topic is broad, it can foster an overall sense of being church and can allow a shared vision to emerge. By contrast, if it is more limited, it can give rise to biased interventions that are not related to the journey of the local church as a whole; at the same time, a more limited topic may allow more in-depth discussion and produce legislation that is more easily achievable.

Second, the role of the bishop remains preponderant, and it may even appear oversized compared to his essential work of guiding the path of the people and legislating for the diocese, as stipulated by the documents and the Code.[40] The study of diocesan synods—their history, the documents they produce, and their reception—shows that they largely depend on the decisions of the individual bishop and that they are only partially received and implemented by his successors. The diocesan synod remains an instrument at the service of the bishop; what is expressed in the assembly is assigned to the sphere of consultation and advice.

On some issues, however, those touching on the ministeriality of the couple or specific areas of pastoral activity, for example, a deliberative vote by the laity would be desirable. In any case, even a merely consultative vote does not mean that the bishop can simply abstain from the ecclesial process in the synod and deliberate freely on his own. Even though the documents protect the prerogatives, freedom, and autonomy of judgment of the bishop, they also remind us that the bishop can distance himself from the opinion expressed by a large part of his church only in serious cases.

As the 1997 Instruction states, there is an "intrinsic connection of the synod with the episcopal function": listening attentively to the Spirit who speaks to and in the local church gathered in the synod allows the bishop to experience himself as a "servant of synodality." As such, he can understand what the best ways are to foster communion and co-responsibility in the church entrusted to him, and he can learn the best ways to exercise his *munus* of father and pastor (see CD 16), as the "one" who makes possible the journey and the unity of the many.

Third, there is the question of representation,[41] which Luca Bressan considers "the point of incandescence, the breaking point of the whole synodal dynamic."[42] The postconciliar synod calls for the widest possible involvement of the baptized, and it also requires listening to those who do not belong to the community but believe they can offer a useful word for the ecclesial journey. The synod's work should be well organized, and it should include moments of wide-ranging listening as well as times of celebration. Some members of the synod will attend by right of office, others will be designated by the bishop, and still others will be chosen by election. With all the members listening to the Spirit, the synodal dynamic will bring about a vital correlation among the bishop, the "some" (the synod members), and "all" the baptized so that, as the 1997 Instruction states, "the members of the synod actively collaborate with their experience and advice in the elaboration of the declarations and decrees."[43] In this sense, the synod is a church event that "makes church" insofar as it favors the maturation of the subjectivity of individuals as well as the maturation of the diocesan church. It is also a "political" event (in the etymological sense of the word) because the members become aware of being an "ecclesial We" as they participate in the elaboration of decisions. It is a church event that takes place through the interaction of all the faithful interpreting the gospel in their operational resumption of the ecclesial mission in the specific local context. Roberto Repole states succinctly that "a synod should offer the possibility of expressing and realizing the subjectivity of the church as a collective subject, created not only by the multiplicity of subjects that co-constitute it, but by the bond of communion that unites them, thus ensuring that the church's destiny is responsibly assumed by the community of believers as a whole."[44] This conception protects against the risk of a "bureaucratic drift" in thinking about representation while making room for the symbolic and epiphanic dimension of the assembly.

In sum, the diocesan synod remains a privileged context for making strategic decisions regarding local church development and the fulfillment of its mission. The synod allows people to experience the power of community discernment and shared deliberation, even with the differences of ministerial roles and responsibilities. The dialogue, confrontation, exchange, and search for consensus foster the growth of a synodal church. The decision-making processes produce, reproduce, and develop social values; they interpret the common history and make all the members aware of what "being We" means, thus creating a "collective culture." Celebrating a synod that invites the contribution of all in understanding the gospel and in searching for joint forms of mission brings with it a reorganization of power relations in the ecclesial institution and a maturing of identity in the laity, as well as in the bishop and the other ordained ministers.

The risk is that the diocesan synod remains an extraordinary event, significant for what the members experience and decide but isolated from the rest of the pastoral life of the diocese. Once the synod's work is concluded and the documents promulgated, the diocese may be only marginally affected by the decisions made. After only a few years, the synod may be remembered by those who participated directly, but in many cases, it will have done little by way of creating a collective memory among the faithful or giving comprehensive guidelines that open a path of community building over time.

Giving continuity to the synod can be done in three ways: (1) working before and during the synodal assembly to create structures of communication and participation that will be maintained afterward; (2) elaborating either a general or a thematic reform project that presents the ideal vision of community and the biblical, theological, and pastoral motivations that guide it; and (3) planning the reception phase and then defining the times, subjects, actions, and structures to be implemented, with a few functional norms for the process. The post–Vatican II synod cannot be reduced simply to a juridical act because deliberation on the pastoral level does not necessarily translate into laws and norms. More importantly, what shapes the mentality and relationships of the participants is the very experience of "doing synod."

As Duffy writes,

> The Church is a pilgrim people. It is in constant search of truth and direction as its members journey together toward their final destiny. They will never have a full understanding of the truth, and often all they can find

is the next step on their way. The Church's synodality is an acknowledgement of this reality: while recognizing that constant reorientation is necessary, it also recognizes that this is done in the company of fellow travelers, with the support of official guides, and, ultimately, under the direction of God's Holy Spirit.[45]

The Diocesan Pastoral Council and the Presbyteral Council

A relevant structural form of participation in the pastoral life of the diocese is the diocesan pastoral council (DPC).[46] The creation of this body is recommended in the decree *Christus Dominus* (27), which states that its specific task is to analyze, discern, and plan pastoral activities. The 2004 Directory for Bishops *Apostolorum Successores* states that the DPC is "an institutional form that expresses the participation of all the faithful … in the mission of the Church" (84). The existence and the mode of work of the DPC depend directly on the bishop, who judges whether it should be established ("if the pastoral situation suggests")[47] and who decides how often it meets[48] and what topics it discusses. The extreme vagueness of these indications has contributed to making this institution extremely fragile. There are widespread complaints about the ineffectiveness and inefficiency of DPCs, and it is evident in many cases that their functioning is weighed down by bureaucratic logic and lacks effectiveness. Various ecclesiological, pastoral, and juridical issues must be addressed so that DPC can become a space for the exercise of ordinary synodality in the local church.

Meeting and Operating Successfully and Efficiently

First, the criteria for identifying the members of DPC should be defined more precisely: the Council refers generically to "clerics, religious and lay people" (CD 27) and states that these can be elected or appointed by the bishop himself. The laity take part by virtue of their baptismal identity, in accord with canons 204 and 208. What is at stake is not just the logic of representing the different associations and "categories" of members involved in pastoral life according to their influence, but also of offering "a kind of image of the community," as the Code of Canon Law suggests by using the verb *configuretur* in canon 512 §2.[49] The activity of the DPC cannot be reduced simply to deliberating on or coordinating pastoral activities: it is a body whose members should take stock of the surrounding social, cultural, and religious reality, and then dialogue on orientations that will guide the path of the local church; all this is done in order to advise the bishop as he exercises his responsibility as pastor of the diocese. The DPC is a body whereby co-responsibility is expressed not only as regards intra-ecclesial life, but more broadly in relation to the church's mission in the larger social context. The agenda of the DPC's work should include reading the signs of the times, identifying the most pressing challenges, recommending specific ecclesial action, and confronting relevant problems. Pope Francis describes this with far-sighted clarity in *Evangelii Gaudium*:

> In his mission of fostering a dynamic, open, and missionary communion, [the bishop] will have to encourage and develop the means of participation proposed in the Code of Canon Law, and other forms of pastoral dialogue, out of a desire to listen to everyone and not simply to those who would tell him what he would like to hear. Yet the principal aim of these participatory processes should not be ecclesiastical organization but rather the missionary aspiration of reaching everyone. (31)

Second, difficulties arise when there is a failure to determine the appropriate relationships and to establish channels of communication between the DPC and the various parishes, associations, and movements. At this time of crisis in representative democracy, when there is less and less appreciation for the right and duty of political participation in the common good by assuming responsibility in trade-union and party-based participatory bodies, in educational institutions, and in local organizations, and when people do not feel represented by those they helped to elect (who, moreover, rarely feel the duty to account for their behavior or even to inform the public about the choices they have made), pastoral councils in the church often also appear exhausted and irrelevant. Particularly in medium- or large-sized dioceses, most of the regular parishioners, pastoral workers, and priests of a diocese do not know the members of the DPC, nor do they receive regular information on what has been discussed. Given the lack of effective coordination between the various levels of the diocese (parish, deanery, curia), the DPC members elected or designated by the bishop end up participating in a personal capacity. Defining very simply the times, the modalities, and the channels of information is the first step to be taken so that synodal forms significantly connect the work of the DPC to the broader path of the local church. Related to this is the second step, which is to identify the times, modalities, and tools with which the DPC or its commissions gather the voices, proposals, and requests that come from the parish bases and lay associations. It would be appropriate, subsequently, to seek the advice of guides who are experts in organizational sociology to make the work more effective by helping the members acquire greater skills in managing time and procedures, in gathering ideas and debate, and in drafting texts.

Moreover, when it is a question of implementing a discernment process or considering decisions that the bishop will have to make, there are limits to being an advisory body with only a "consultative vote," which the bishop can accept or reject without having to justify his behavior.[50] The Code of Canon Law is undoubtedly oriented toward protecting the bishop's freedom of choice: he is not to be bound in any way in the exercise of his ministry by the recommendations of the DPC, even when they represent the majority view. There are, however, matters in which the laity are competent to make a substantially binding decision, leaving the bishop with the option of exercising his veto right and asking for further discussion, after seeking and receiving the opinion of experts and theologians. While it is not the laity's task to preside over the DPC (the one who presides over the local church should do so, in service to the "ecclesial We" that is proper to him by virtue of his ministry), one of the laity can be entrusted with the task of coordinating the work, thus transferring to the diocesan level what A. Borras argues for the parish level:

> Distinguishing coordination from presidency guarantees the effectiveness of the former and the credibility of the latter because in the pastoral council, just as in the Eucharist and in the rest of [parish] life, the parish priest must not do everything and say everything; rather, he must ensure that all parishioners have a chance to speak and that everything gets done.

Thus, the DPC agenda could be jointly decided by the presiding bishop and the lay coordinator, leaving the council members free to propose, with a deliberative vote, the topics to be discussed and the working methods.

Finally, as Vito Mignozzi points out, the DPC could be given a specific role in the selection of bishops to lead the local church, so as to ensure continuity in the diocesan path.[51] The

DPC could indicate to the bishops of the region and to the nuncio of the country the characteristics considered necessary and desirable in the new bishop, and it could inform the new bishop, once named, about the diocesan pastoral project and the motivations that guided its drafting so that he understands well the steps already taken and has an adequate understanding of the present pastoral needs. Of course, as the ITC document on synodality states, the DPC can "offer a qualified contribution to the overall pastoral approach promoted by the Bishop and his *presbyterium*; on occasions it also becomes a place for decisions under the specific authority of the Bishop." The DPC is therefore "the most appropriate permanent structure for implementing synodality in the local Church."[52] It is the space in which, on the one hand, the "some" truly offer a service to the "one" bishop in the local church and, on the other, they enable participation of the different components of the people of God in bringing about change in perspectives and ideas.

Priests, the Bishop's First Co-operators

Similar considerations apply to the functioning of the diocesan presbyteral council.[53] *Christus Dominus* 27 briefly refers to possible *consilia*, which are made up only of priests who cooperate with the bishop in the government of the diocese (expressly mentioned are the cathedral chapter and the college of consultors). We also find a more precise indication in *Presbyterorum Ordinis* 7, where the bishops are exhorted to establish,[54] "in a manner suited to today's conditions and necessities, and with a structure and norms to be determined by law, a body or senate of priests representing all the priests. This representative body by its advice will be able to give the bishop effective assistance in the administration of the diocese." The document further states that the bishops "should gladly listen to their priests, indeed consult them and engage in dialogue with them in those matters which concern the necessities of pastoral work and welfare of the diocese." It is the duty of bishops to "consult" the priests assembled in a body that is not merely consultative:[55] the decree uses the adverb *efficaciter* and the verb *adiuvare* to define the body's contribution.

The presbyteral council "can be said to be [acting] 'synodally'; while leaving the bishop the final word, the priests will study together with the bishop the issues related to the particular church's mission in that place and time and will offer the orientations deemed appropriate, which the bishop must take into due consideration."[56] This perspective is also adopted in the document of the International Theological Commission, which stresses that the presbyteral council is a "permanent body for the exercise and promotion of communion and synodality" and that it "has a specific place in the local Church's overall synodal dynamic, whose spirit animates it and whose style shapes it."[57] This statement describes well the peculiar nature of this body, and it highlights the special relationship that exists between the bishop and the presbyterate. A. Borras goes so far as to speak of a "devolution of power."[58]

The challenge here, once again, is to provide an effective organizational and communicational structure, so that the discussions of the presbyteral council involve all the priests of the diocese and yield fruit more immediately for the pastoral life of the diocese and not only indirectly through the word and action of the bishop who takes the advice of a few representative priests.

A SYNODAL PARISH

While certainly not the only institution which evangelizes, if the parish proves capable of constant self-renewal and adaptivity, it continues to be "the Church living in the midst of the homes of her sons and daughters." This presumes that the parish really is in contact with the homes and the lives of its people, and does not become a useless structure out of touch with people or a self-absorbed group made up of a chosen few. (EG 28)

With these words from *Evangelii Gaudium*, Pope Francis urges the renewal of the parish with respect to its participatory style, its pastoral proposals, and its formation structures. The parish remains an important ecclesial figure because it is the one closest to the experience of most of the faithful; it can accompany people in the meaningful moments of their lives and guarantee to all the gifts of sacramental grace and basic formation. Nevertheless, the parish today appears to be in difficulty because, as it faces the challenges posed by the new social and cultural context, it often fails to conform fully to the ecclesial and ecclesiological model proposed by Vatican II.[59] In fact, regarding pastoral practice and the common understanding, the old conception of parish received from the past remains unchanged in many respects, thus making overall ecclesial renewal difficult.[60]

The model of parish developed after the Council of Trent was born in and for a context of *societas christiana*, that is, an environment that was socioculturally and religiously homogeneous. Being conceived primarily for the *cura animarum* and the preservation of the faith, the parish centered on the religious socialization of children and the sacramentalization and doctrinal formation of adults and young people. The priest was at the center of the parish as the full subject, while the laity were considered recipients or "consumers" of religious services or, at most, as collaborators of the clergy in the apostolate and in the witness of their lives. This model of parish was structured around communicational and decision-making processes that worked from the top down, from the clergy to the laity, from the adult to the child, from the male to the female, from those who had knowledge and ability (because they had theological speech, sacred power, and jurisdiction) to those who had neither power nor knowledge; in effect, from the "one" to the "all."

The parish today must move toward a synodal form and structure of relations to implement more fully the ecclesiology of Vatican II. The coordinates for such a change come from the sociocultural and religious context. Urbanization, the third industrial revolution, and the ongoing digital revolution have changed people's relationship to space and time and territorial references. Latter-day secularization is witnessing a return of religion to the public sphere, but it is combined with the desire of individuals to develop a personal style of belief and ecclesial belonging. Increased mobility and migration favor religious and cultural pluralism, disrupting older contexts of homogeneous social belonging.

Christians today, even in Europe, find that they are in a minority, the Catholic Church being just one of the many subjects that speak out in the public sphere. All these factors give rise to new participatory "grassroots" dynamics that are at work in the complex task of reorganizing essential institutions, including the church. Such dynamics help institutions to become "lighter" and more agile so that they can guarantee transparency and encourage a pluralistic, inclusive sense of belonging without precluding engagement with other vital environments and without demanding binding and exclusive adherence.[61]

Multidirectional Relations of
Communication and Participation

Even though the "models" of parishes have always varied,[62] thinking today about a "parish in synodal form" requires rethinking what the main features of parishes have always been: evangelization, presence in a defined territory, and eucharistic community. The parish as institution was formed around these three features from the fourth century on, first in the countryside and later in the cities. To ensure these three elements, the forms of relationship, presence, and pastoral action have changed over the centuries. Based on these essential elements, the tasks now are to inculturate the parish in the dynamics of contemporary society, to "streamline" the many religious activities and services of the standardized Tridentine model, and to "redesign" the dynamics that shape the many faces of parish community so that they are able to proclaim the gospel in a meaningful way. The parish must make itself prophetically present in its territory, assuming responsibility and celebrating communion with God and among people in an authentic, nonsacralized way.

The process that generates and regenerates the church develops around the gospel proclaimed and understood, the gospel celebrated and lived by all the *christifideles*, with their wealth of charisms and ministries by which the Spirit leads the church in its life and mission. For this reason, the rediscovery of synodality as a constitutive dimension of the church and the promotion of synodal dynamics as a particular way of living and acting in the church are at the heart of the now urgent task of parish renewal. The parish model necessarily changes when we consider the contributions of the various subjects with their diverse roles and functions. The new pastoral dynamics will be expressed in ways that allow the collective subject "church" to be recognized. As the center of gravity shifts away from the clergy, sacramentalizing activities, and a centripetal dynamic, the focus will be instead on co-responsibility in a ministerial church, adult evangelization, and vital engagement with the human territory. From being directed by "one" (the parish priest) together with "some" lay collabora-tors, the parish will move on to a complex sharing dynamic of synergy that promotes collaboration among the "all," the "many" with their diverse ministries and skills, and the "one" (ordained minister), who is called to be a "servant of the synodal path."

The force driving synodal change is to be found in the pro-motion and structuring of multidirectional relations of commu-nication and participation, in accord with *Lumen Gentium* 12 and *Dei Verbum* 8, thus overcoming the Gregorian-Tridentine model of church in which communication is unidirectional, from one to all and from center to periphery.[63] All subjects are given their proper place so that they can speak their word, share their under-standing of the gospel, express their opinions and judgments on the pastoral choices to be made, and listen to what is shared by all the other church subjects. Relationships in the church are asym-metrical: ordained ministers, in their constitutive service to the institutionalized "ecclesial We," have a specific and indispens-able word in the communicational dynamics that make up the church; they make a unique contribution that cannot be equated with that of the other faithful. Ordained to serve the *consensus fidelium* and safeguard the *sensus fidei ecclesiae*, these ministers must promote and nourish the many diverse, multidirectional communicational dynamics that foster a mature ecclesial con-science, shared decision-making, and participatory forms of litur-gical celebration. Similarly, the discernment of the charisms of the baptized, the promotion of the ministerial role of laypeople, the coordination of pastoral activities, and the setting of general guidelines for the life of the community are all expressions of the ordained ministers' service and the presidency of the "one" in and for the "ecclesial We." This asymmetry must be guaranteed, but without returning to hierarchical or kyriarchical schemes that poison ecclesial relations.

The Postconciliar Reception

As is well known, the Council documents say little about the parish, and then only indirectly, in relation to other themes; they do not offer a definition or a systematic description.[64] The wider horizon of the Council's ecclesiology, however, allows and requires a rethinking of the nature of the parish in the postconciliar church, and the documents highlight some of its essential elements. The parish is a local community defined by a territory and led by a pastor who is concerned for the *salus animarum* (CD 30–31); it is a *coetus fidelium* forming a cell (AA 10) that is a part (CD 30–32) of the diocese. In a certain way (*quodammodo*), the parish represents the universal church (SC 42) and is committed to the task of prophetic witness (AG 37) and community apostolate (AA 10); it is characterized by the community celebration of the Eucharist (SC 42).

Synodal reform of the parish in terms of its structures and *forma ecclesiae* is based not only on the Council decrees but also and especially on the few but significant passages from pontifical magisterial documents and the pastoral letters of local bishops, including the recent instruction drawn up by the Congregation for the Clergy.[65]

The ecclesial community, while always having a universal dimension, finds its most immediate and visible expression in the parish. It is there that the Church is seen locally. In a certain sense it is the Church living in the midst of the homes of her sons and daughters. It is necessary that in light of the faith all rediscover the true meaning of the parish, that is, the place where the very "mystery" of the Church is present and at work, even if at times it is lacking persons and means, even if at other times it might be scattered over vast territories or almost not to be found in crowded and chaotic modern sections of cities. The parish is not principally a structure, a territory, or a building, but rather, "the family of God, a fellowship afire with a unifying spirit" (LG 28), "a familial and welcoming home" (CT 67), the "community of the faithful" (can. 515). Plainly and simply, the parish is founded on a theological reality, because it is a Eucharistic community.[66]

This perspective yields certain criteria that should guide the synodal configuration of the parish, this peculiar and irreplaceable form of ecclesial life. Every decision on the organizational level and every structure should express and promote the nature of the parish as a community, with a stress on hearing the Word of God, being actively present in a specified territory, providing various services, offering prophetic witness, and celebrating Eucharist. The parish as an inclusive community is anti-elitist; the only criteria for belonging are the profession of faith, baptism, and residence in a specific territory. The parish encourages the active co-responsibility of all the faithful, both men and women, who can contribute to building up the community with their word and their service, according to their own charisms and ministries.

Thus, the challenge is to activate a synergistic dynamic of participation that allows the community's identity to be experienced as closely related to the people's lives and the needs of the territory, and to do so in a way that corresponds to the local culture. As Severino Dianich writes,

> The full figure of the church, the true people of God, is found where the ecclesial congregation adheres closely to the population of a place, welcoming all its expressions, values, and even its miseries. Such is the parish community....The population of the place offers the church its human material and its basic fabric, and the Christian community, defined by a territory, remains essentially linked to the population of the territory. In this sense, the parish community is necessarily conditioned by the specific culture of the people, and its mission is determined by the first and principal interlocutor of its proclamation and dialogue, which is precisely the population of the area in which it lives.[67]

The territorial reference can no longer be the one established in the second millennium: in many countries of the world today, the residence of individuals does not coincide with the many places in which they spend their lives—workplace, recreation, friendships, family of origin. In a modern context that makes it easy to move freely and to choose the social settings that one wishes; the post-Tridentine parish (not yet structurally reshaped by Vatican II) appears obsolete because it cannot encompass the spheres of social interaction not linked to the home. It therefore denies people the freedom to belong to religious communities of their choice, which are not necessarily founded on the principle of territoriality (consider the various associations and movements of laypeople). The traditional parish appears to be defined by a principle linked to functional relationships and by the provision of religious services rather than by the truth of interpersonal relationships in faith and mutual love.

Certainly, the criterion of residence attests to the reality of the parish as a place of "shared" faith that does not require a specific spirituality, a high level of doctrinal knowledge, or a radical approach to living the faith. The parish is truly a non-elitist institution that is open to all and guarantees inclusion, allowing everyone to experience being part of God's people. But this criterion cannot be the only reference today. As adults, we want to avoid being nomads; we want to belong to a specific local community and take public responsibility for the shared journey in an ongoing way. At the same time, we want to recognize our relationship with the territory by being visibly present as the "We that is parish community," by being responsible for the evangelization of that human space, by responding to its needs through the practice of charity, and by helping all to grow in shared faith and Christian solidarity.

The Role of the Parish Priest

It is evident, today more than ever, that the parish is at a crossroads between the two dynamics of ecclesial life: the free choice of those who make up the parish (of which we are aware once again) and the institutional momentum (a church born from the proclamation of faith and living by relationships of communion), or, to put it differently, between personal Christian experience and life as part of a collective body. The parish provides the faithful with the opportunity to have deep and meaningful relationships, to interweave their own thoughts with those of others in understanding the gospel, and to share their own charisms and exercise their own ministry in the vital daily experience of formation, celebration, and service.

The parish allows an indispensable synodal sense to mature, making it available to all. The members of a parish experience real community despite differences of gender, age, and interest and despite the diverse conditions of life and experiences of faith that are proper to the people of God. The parish that becomes a true sign of loving communion will have a strong impact on the surrounding social environment (see AA 10). As the primary space for synodal life, the parish community provides the faithful with a genuine opportunity to experience mutual recognition, to be enriched by giving generously of their time and skills, and to engage in direct dialogue and discussion with others, without any need for complex mechanisms of representation and delegation. For parish renewal to take place in a synodal perspective, participatory bodies such as the pastoral council and the council for economic affairs must obviously be reactivated.[68] It is also very important to rethink the role of the parish priest and the way in which he coordinates with the other pastoral workers and the more active community members. Likewise, internal reorganization is needed in the ecclesial base communities and the small domestic communities.

Christus Dominus 30 describes the role of the parish priest, first in terms of the relationships (to the bishop, other priests, the faithful, lay pastoral cooperators, parish vicars) that define his figure and his service and then in terms of the functions and tasks that are proper to him as the *pastor proprius* responsible for the *cura animarum* of the community entrusted to him.[69] Although the conciliar text has many traits of continuity with the Tridentine vision and with the 1917 Code of Canon Law that was in force at the time, it offers several new elements: it presents the proclamation of the gospel as the main principle of ecclesial dynamics; it envisions community life as expressed and realized in the liturgy, especially the Eucharist; it reaffirms the subjectivity of the laity;

and it places the parish within the horizon of the local church (as "*pars dioecesis*"). However, the text does not escape from an interpretative framework of community life centered on the parish priest: he is the "one" who exercises practically every power of orientation and decision-making in the community, without prejudice to the bishop.

As *pastor proprius* (a juridical term, not a metaphor), the priest has his own ordinary (undelegated) governing power, which he exercises in his own name. He does not act independently of the bishop: he is a pastor with the bishop and under his authority; he is appointed by the bishop; his pastoral action is subject to the bishop's direction; and he is accountable only to the bishop for his decisions. In serving the common priesthood of the faithful, he is a teacher who proclaims the Word of God and provides catechesis; he is moved by "fatherly charity," which translates into loving care and creative pastoral proposals; he is urged to cooperate with religious and laypeople and to encourage the community's cooperation so that he is not the only one engaged in direct action. However, there is no getting away from the perspective that he is the initiator of every communication and every decision and that the parishioners are basically the recipients of his words and decisions.[70]

For a synodal parish community, the role of the parish priest needs to be rethought so that there is a sharing of the powers that today are all concentrated in his person; he needs to be relieved of those tasks and functions that can be taken on by competent, trained laypeople. With a view to evaluating and verifying the priest's work, there is a need to establish forms that are not currently compulsory but are essential for the quality of community life, such as joint pastoral planning and economic and administrative management of the parish. Priests who, by mandate of the bishop, take on responsibility for a parish should receive prior training in transformational and cooperative leadership so that they can guide the complex processes of community life. They should not be limited, as was the case with the Tridentine parish priests, to immediate personal relationships with individual parishioners or to proposing and coordinating pastoral activities. As we saw in the previous chapter, there can be no lay cooperation or exercise of ecclesial co-responsibility unless the priest can delegate and coordinate pastoral agents, unless he can have trust in his coworkers and recognize their equal baptismal dignity, and unless he values the skills of other members of the community. The synergy of "one, some, and all" must mark the life of the parish community especially, and it is the task of the parish priest to promote and guarantee that synergy.

Sharing the Faith

Second, work is needed on the parish's internal configuration so that the synodal spirit has adequate spaces and instruments by which to be embodied among the faithful.[71] "Small Christian Communities"[72] in Africa and "Basic Ecclesial Communities"[73] are the most interesting examples of parish reconfiguration. Based on the experience of faith-sharing among adults, they provide a good alternative to the structuring of the Tridentine parish. We will focus on the Basic Ecclesial Communities (BECs) and the impact they have had in the churches of Latin America and Europe. "The grassroots ecclesial communities have been and are a gift from God to the local churches of Amazonia." With these words of the Final Document of the Synod (36), the bishops of Amazonia acknowledged the decisive contribution that the BECs have made to ecclesial life in their region over the last fifty years. Arising in Latin America during the 1960s, first in Brazil, they were mentioned in the 1968 Medellín Document as a primary instrument of evangelization and ecclesial renewal, fully in accord with the inculturation called for by Vatican II.

The Medellín conference recommended the formation of "the greatest possible number of ecclesial communities in parishes, especially in rural areas and poor urban districts. These communities should be based on the Word of God and should participate as much as possible in the celebration of the Eucharist, always in communion with and under the direction of the bishop."[74] These elements were subsequently developed in other general conferences of the Latin American bishops in Puebla (1979), Santo Domingo (1992), and Aparecida (2007). The BECs were declared to be "a way of being church and expressing the church";[75] their style and purpose were described as similar to those of the first Christian communities.[76] As one of the most original experiences of the Latin American churches, the BECs were "centers of evangelization and engines of liberation and development";[77] they constituted the "initial cells of ecclesial restructuring and the focal points of faith and evangelization."[78]

Christian Formation and the Struggle for Justice

The experience of the BECs, involving hundreds of thousands of the faithful, profoundly affected the life of the Latin American churches, and it influenced the configuration of parishes and dioceses, even in remote Amazonia. The Final Document of the Amazon Synod relates this reflection to the challenges of urban pastoral care, but the reflection also applies to rural areas and the rainforest, to all places where small communities meet regularly for liturgical celebration. The celebration may be eucharistic if a priest is present, or it may be led by laypeople, deacons, or sisters if no priest can preside. The BECs are the presence of the church in the territory; they hear the Word of God even as they closely examine the social reality around them. They are spaces where people are formed in a faith that is incarnated and prophetic, a faith that is able both to announce and to denounce.

The struggle for justice and the defense of basic rights for all—water, housing, energy, citizenship—depend, say the bishops, on the capillary action of the BECs operating in the urban slums and the *villas miserias*. Emboldened by faith that is fully aware of the social dimension of the gospel, they know how to make Christian charity a political force. In *Querida Amazonia* 96, Pope Francis describes these grassroots communities as vital experiences of synodality in evangelization. Citing the Aparecida Document (178), he highlights the contribution they have made "to the formation of Christians who, steeped in the faith, are missionary disciples of the Lord." He insists that such communities are an essential condition for "integrating the defense of social rights with missionary proclamation and spirituality."

A Way to Reform the Church

These short passages dedicated to the grassroots communities in Amazonia are quite valuable and relevant also for the churches in Europe and elsewhere in the world.

In its Final Document, the synod expressed its desire to accept the Council's challenge to become a renewed missionary church, a desire that Latin American bishops have expressed from Medellín onward. They understood that any reform of the church must start from listening to the gospel in the different cultures—a principle that generates and regenerates the church—and it must envisage humanly dimensioned forms of community life that make it possible for everyone to communicate in faith, participate actively, and celebrate fruitfully.

The rapid spread in the postconciliar period of this at once new and ancient reality, the BECs, has led to a revision of the traditional categories of ecclesial self-awareness so that parishes are increasingly thought of as "communities of communities." As the Aparecida Document asserts, "the renewal of parishes at the beginning of the third millennium requires their structures to be reorganized so that they become a network of communities and groups capable of developing in such a way as to ensure that the members feel, and really are, disciples and missionaries of Jesus Christ."[79] The preference given to the "bases" has played an essential role in rethinking the church, which is now seen to be a church that lives and works in everyday places, a church that is above all a church of the poor and for the poor, and a church that is truly universal and inclusive.

The BECs, which are not simply an instrument of pastoral strategy, are proof that the church can and must "reinvent itself" institutionally. It must create for itself new structures and organizational methods in which laypeople are truly the primary subjects of "doing church." The BECs make it possible for people to experience themselves as a "We in community" and as related to a particular territory, an essential element of being church but one that often remains in the background. The smaller number of members in the BECs allows for a shared hearing of the Word, easier communication, mutual recognition, and a sense of co-responsibility. BECs help people to abandon anonymity and to create a network of relationships of mutual help and support. The organizational autonomy of the BECs can provide all the elements needed for the maturation of adult believers and for the formation of community subjects who are authentic but are usually thought of as secondary in traditional pastoral life.

"Rooted in the heart of the world, they [the BECs] are privileged spaces for living the faith in community; they are sources of fraternity and solidarity, providing an alternative to today's society, which is based on selfishness and ruthless competition."[80] Precisely because the BECs in their habitual way of life unite formation and action, celebration and service, proclamation of liberation and transformation of society, they can teach the universal church how to achieve the desired reform. Reform will not happen as the result of a decision from above, nor will it consist simply of replacing outdated structures with new, more modern ones. Reform will happen only through the slow, participatory steps of all the components of the people of God, starting from those who are "less able" precisely because they are less recognized in the eyes of the world.

The option for a synodal parish requires us to start again from the core of community life. United in a "community of mutual sympathy," people experience the truth of a dynamic relation that is born of and nourished by multidirectional communicational dynamics that respect the charisms, ministries, and sensibilities of every member.[81] A parish that is a "community of communities" is a cell of the synodal church, as is shown by the eucharistic dynamic celebrated there. If in the small communities the shared hearing of the gospel generates and shapes relationships of faith in a form that can then be shared by all, then the parish expresses—when a priest presides, and the Eucharist is celebrated—the form of being a people in relation to a territory.

DECISION-MAKING IN THE CHURCH

The synodal dimension touches the *forma ecclesiae*, the ways in which the faithful participate and communicate at the community level, as well as the ways in which structures and processes are organized. The decision-making dynamic is thus central to achieving synodality.[82] Niklas Luhmann writes that "every organization is operationally made up of decisions,"[83] and the church, like every other organization, operates through decisions.

A Church That Decides in a Synodal Manner

As we explained in the first chapters of this book, synodality does not give rise to forms of parliamentary democracy or to a system that delegates powers to a few so that they can govern the public realm for a period in defined areas. Rather, synodality is understood in the Catholic Church in the framework of differentiated subjectivities, namely, laypeople and ordained ministers (in the first place, bishops, and then, according to their specific ministerial role, priests and deacons).

While they are all recognized as co-constituent subjects of the church and therefore co-participants in the realization of the synodal dynamics (see *Lumen Gentium*, chapter II), they are recognized as such according to differentiated, asymmetrical relationships of communication, participation, and decision-making. In other words, their common identity as *christifideles* is marked by different charisms and ministries, while their specific identities are marked by different sacramental foundations. While their messianic mission is the same (see LG 9) and their dignity as ecclesial subjects is the same (see LG 32), the ways in which they contribute to the life and action of the church in the world are different (see AA 2; LG 32, 37).

Any reflection on deliberative processes in the church and on the synodally defined form that they can and must take today is rooted in recognition of this differentiated membership between ordained ministers and the laity, ordered to the constitution and the action of the "ecclesial We." It is also rooted in the dynamism envisaged in *Lumen Gentium* 12, which describes the contribution that the individual *fideles* make, by their faith and profession of faith, to what is common (*sensus fidei ecclesiae*). The maturation of the *sensus fidei* comes about through the achievement of a *consensus fidelium* in the interaction between what comes from "all" and what is guaranteed by the "one," the ordained minister who is the promoter and guardian of the *consensus*.[84]

The realization of a church as the people of God, as outlined in the Council's Constitution on the Church, is achieved when effective multidirectional communicative and participative dynamics are guaranteed, even in decision-making. All the baptized can participate in such dynamics, even while preserving the asymmetrical form of elaborative/interpretative and deliberative/decision-making relationships that unite the church in a synergy of differentiated contributions from ordained ministers and the laity. The two key concepts on which we insist when speaking of synodality—namely, "co-responsibility" and "participation" (in the double sense of "being part" and "taking part")—cannot be adequately achieved without addressing the question of the renewal decision-making dynamics. As A. Borras writes, the exercise of (personal) authority is marked at the present time by insufficient consideration of the *sensus fidei* of the faithful, by excessive concentration of power, by an isolated exercise of authority, by a centralized and discretionary style of governance, by opaque regulatory procedures, and by nonexistent accountability.[85] Real transformation is needed also on this level.

Reflection on decision-making in the church and as a church requires a significant overcoming of the "hierarchical pyramidal" model, which is characterized by a mainly unidirectional communicative and participative dynamic. This centralized decision-making model is centered on the power of the "one" who decides for "all," sometimes with the contribution of intermediate cadres, the "some" who will implement the decisions made. Synodality requires accepting a communal model of church in which decisions are made in the network of communicative, asymmetrical relationships. Such a network recognizes all the faithful as hearers of the Word of God through the words of others (see DV 10), and it recognizes all as competent voices regarding decisions that concern the ecclesial body. It therefore must truly involve everyone, though in differentiated forms.

Making Decisions

Like any other institution, the church is also continually involved in making decisions.[86] Every organization, to achieve its goal, needs to decide how to operate. It does not know the future and must always consider new facts and events that affect it from both within and without.[87] Moreover, "decisions mark the difference between the past and the future that they themselves produce."[88] They develop the collective consciousness and shape the form of the church; indeed, when and how we make decisions defines who we are. How can we rethink "deciding" so that it is an authentic *expression* of the synodal church and *contributes to the maturation* of consciousness and to the *effective praxis* of the church as the people of God? How can we move beyond the linear two-step scheme that currently characterizes the church's decision-making process: "consultation (of the laity) and deliberation (of the bishops/priests)"?

At present, in fact, the "one" controls the information, indicates the general orientations, decides the necessary steps, and supervises the decision-making processes. The "one" decides whether to make decisions (either alone or involving others, according to his inclination) or not to make decisions (and perhaps prevent others from making them as well). The laypeople, the "all," are seen as implementers of what is decided, or at best as advisors. The dynamics of a synodal church, as envisaged by

the conciliar ecclesiology, involve instead the constitutive interaction of communication and decision-making among several
subjects—the "one," the "some" (priests, pastoral agents), and the
"all"—so that the prophetic and royal *munera* of the baptized (see
LG 12) are correlated with the exercise of the *munera docendi,
regendi ac pascendi* (LG 25, 27; CD 16) of the ordained ministers.

The early church made its own Justinian's principle of law:
"*quod omnes tangit, ab omnibus tractari (et approbari) debet.*"[89] This
principle requires that the complex decision-making processes be
organized in several phases during which the different ministerial
subjects interact and share their various contributions. There can
be no real synodality without a substantial revision of the dynamics and structures of decision-making. The strategies for arriving
at decisions must be studied, and the existing structural mechanisms and those that can be activated need to be understood. In
all this, it is important to bear in mind the "symbolic" and not
just the functional importance of the decision-making process for
the social body. In the "cooperative system" that is the church,
decisions must emerge from the interaction of all elements: individuals who contribute based on their personal experience, committed groups and associations, and the exercise of the ordained
ministry.

Whatever the nature of the decision-making—strategic
choices in overall planning, operational matters, the program-
ming of activities, or particular problems—the sociology of organizations and the research on decision-making can offer valuable
suggestions.[90] In fact, acquiring skills in problem solving and
creative thinking allows for decisions to be made in a way that
is more meaningful and more consistent with the purpose of the
institution. Such a process of practical thinking contributes to the
maturation of the identity of the collective subject involved.

A Multistage Decision-Making Process
Supporting Decision-Taking

Sociologists show us that deciding can be conceived as a multistep process in which it is possible to identify the sequence of phases by which a decision is reached. Decision-making (the progressive five-phase maturation of the decision) can be distinguished from decision-taking (the deliberative moment). The differentiated involvement of the "one," the "some," and the "all" can be indicated for each phase of decision-making, in accord with the "co-essentiality between hierarchical and charismatic gifts."[91]

Decision-making

1	• defining/clarifying the issue of the decision	one → some
2	• collect data and information	all · some
3	• outlining the possible alternatives for enacting	some → many
4	• identifying "criteria of evaluation/discernment"	theologians · one
5	• evaluating the different alternatives	all · some
6	• Decision-taking	votes · one

all · some
one

1. First, *the object of the decision must be defined and clarified*. The "one," the parish priest or bishop, can involve the people of God in the process of deliberation, but this convocation can also be solicited by "many" of the faithful through an expression of unease or desire that the "one" perceives, or it can be expressly requested by "some" collaborators. Sometimes a minority can point out existing difficulties and problems. The first task, then, is to clearly identify the matter to be discussed and to delimit it so that it can be discussed effectively.

2. The second step is to *gather relevant information about the choice to be made*, both by involving and listening to *all* the faithful and by soliciting specific contributions from *some* (priests, pastoral offices and commissions, pastoral agents). Knowledge and skills come together with the life experiences and faith reflections of the many or the all: the larger the number of those involved, the broader and deeper the understanding of the problem or issue being decided. It is essential that the church listen to the *laity* for their reading of reality and their judgment in the light of the gospel proclamation; their highly diverse formative and life experiences will widen the perspective and increase the information. The faithful are to be consulted by virtue of their baptismal condition (Code of Canon Law, cc. 204, 208) and their charisms and skills (c. 112 §3).

3. It is then a question of *delineating the alternatives* that are effective and feasible. There should be several alternatives, unlike what usually happens, and

they should be feasible. In other words, it should be possible for each of the possible choices to pass from "could" to "should" to "must" to "we must," thus guaranteeing that the action of the ecclesial body will be effective. In this phase of *decision-making*, the "*some*" (for example, pastoral workers, ordained ministers, and laypeople; theologians; psychologists and sociologists) have the basic role of "thinking differently" with respect to the present situation or what is already known. Combining creative thinking and rational logic to tackle the problems, they have the task of imagining the transitions to be made, planning the operational sequences to be activated, and evaluating the possible consequences.

4. At this point it is necessary to *identify the "criteria of judgment"* that will allow a choice to be made that is consistent with the purpose and style of the church's mission. On the one hand, it is the task of theologians—in the light of scripture and tradition—to indicate and recall some guiding principles; on the other hand, it is the word of the bishop himself, with his priests and deacons, that *gathers* whatever preserves the apostolicity of the faith in the concrete situation. It is up to the bishop to present these criteria to all the faithful, motivating them to draw on their strength and inspirational orientation for ecclesial action.

5. The community can be asked to *assess* the various alternatives according to the indicated "criteria of judgment" so that those actions and guidelines are chosen that appear most appropriate in the light

of the gospel and the signs of the times. Here, too, the competencies of the laity are crucial. The judgment regarding the preferability of the various options can be expressed either by surveying the broad consensus or by voting. All should be asked to express their views (sometimes publicly) with respect to the options proposed, and an assessment should be made of the general orientation of the ecclesial body and the breadth and depth of the consensus.

6. The process of "elaborating and evaluating the question" that is carried out in these phases sustains the last necessary step: *decision-taking* by the pastoral authority. The decision of the "one," the ordained minister, is not simply a ratification of the decision-making process developed up to this point. Rather, it is an expression of his specific ministry of safeguarding the apostolicity of the faith and serving the "ecclesial We"; he does this by discerning what the community has indicated as a result of thorough research and honest assessment based on evangelical criteria. Gathering the voices, he progressively leads the church toward a *consensus* that becomes the expression of the "ecclesial We" (which is not the sum of opinions or the expression of a parliamentary majority). This is precisely the service of those who exercise the presidency in the community: they formalize and legitimize what has progressively emerged. Theodore of Mopsuestia described the process well in a delightfully concise expression: "the minister is the common language of the church." It will be the bishop or

the parish priest, then, who delivers the decision taken to "all" the faithful and to the "some" (pastoral workers) so that it can be implemented. As bishops and parish priests, the ministers will then have to evaluate the adequacy of the implementation with respect to the decision taken, ensuring that the reasons and the instances of service that motivated the choice are preserved. The reception and implementation of a decision are, after all, part of the process of discernment: the selection of elements, the broadening of perspectives, and the experience of unforeseen implications contribute to defining the value and the meaning of what has been decided together.

The vote expressed by the laity has a consultative value (c. 514 §1),[92] so that the bishop is free to accept or not accept what has been voted on in a diocesan synod. He is not "bound by any obligation to accept their vote" (c. 127 §2b), although he can depart from it only for serious reasons of conscience (c. 127 §2b).[93] The long process of discernment is, in any case, an expression of the co-responsibility of all the components of the people of God as participants in the prophetic and royal *munera* of Christ. The vote taken—especially if unanimous or by a large majority—expresses their collective judgment on reality and on pastoral orientation; in a certain way, therefore, it binds the bishop "in conscience" and should guide all his discernment.

An Excessively Complicated Process?

The decision-making structure in the church must become increasingly articulated, "polymorphous," and flexible, capable of generating new ideas, mutual stimulation, common experiences, and constructive criticism. It must engender a sense of belonging and allow everyone to contribute to the common work (the *synphèron* of 1 Cor 12:7). The constantly evolving life of the church today is confronted with the new challenges posed by the times and the changing culture. These challenges show the need for overcoming the standardized procedures used in the Tridentine parish model. We must think instead of new approaches and differentiated responses to the present-day problems, making use of the strategic interaction of the skills of the laity, which are many and diverse. Even if the decision-making process described above appears overly complex or too slow in its response to the challenges, it possesses two unquestionable benefits: first, it involves many people (if not all); and second, the faithful will be more motivated to act the more they have been involved in the decision-making process and know the reasons for the decisions made. The process is one that develops in real coherence with the nature of the "ecclesial We"—communion in and through communication of the faith. People cannot be a community if they do not participate in the decision-making that affects the social body.

What counts in every decision-making process is not only the problem solved (what has been decided, the product of decision-taking/-making), but also the way in which discernment is done: the interactions that have taken place, the meaning that has emerged, and the consciousness that has matured. In deliberative processes, there is always a symbolic construction at stake: not only is the synodal form of diocese or parish expressed in this model of community discernment, but it progressively matures precisely through the experiences of deliberation conducted in this way. Still another reason for engaging in integrated *decision-making* is that it allows us to address the *gender gap* that exists today. In the Catholic Church, women can contribute only as part of the "all" and the "some" (as pastoral workers, theologians, members of pastoral councils, and so forth). They cannot contribute as "one," that is, as an ordained minister in service to the community.

The guarantee of the apostolicity of the faith and the presidency of the community cannot be exercised by women. Very few women, either lay and religious, participate in ecclesial *decision-making*; they exercise little authority or influence over the direction of community life and activity. What kind of cooperative leadership is possible in an institution in which the power of representation and decision-making is almost exclusively in the hands of males? Only an integrated process of decision-making can preserve the authoritative word of women, enhance their contribution on the basis of their experience and competence, and at the same time promote reflection on authority and power in the church from the perspective of gender.

Synodality and Leadership in Decision-Making Processes

"Let the bishop decide nothing without the advice of the priests and the suffrage of all the people."[94] At each stage of the decision-making process, the service exercised by the "one," the ordained minister who presides over the discerning community, is essential.[95] It is the "one" who summons everyone for community discernment, defines the pastoral action to be discussed in terms of its goal, and clearly presents the question (phase 1). Next, he accompanies the process by listening to everyone (phases 2, 3, 5) and ensuring that all the baptized are heard. He encourages those with pastoral charisms, skills, and responsibilities to make their contribution, guaranteeing free discussion, allowing spaces for creativity, and pointing out the limits of all the "actors" involved, including his own.

His primary tasks, by virtue of the gift of the Spirit he has received, are to explain clearly the evangelical criteria for judging the various options (phase 4) and then to take the final decision (phase 6). In doing so, he should synthesize for the community the fruit of discernment, being careful not to isolate his own task of *decision-taking* from the broader, more inclusive process of *decision-making*. It is his responsibility to declare the "consensus reached," which is never a simple ratification of what has been expressed or voted on by the community; rather, it involves a further step of ministerial discernment that is the fruit of the Spirit. It is therefore his responsibility to speak on behalf of the "ecclesial We" and to deliver the decision reached so that it can be actively received by the community.[96]

It is in this way that the bishop and the parish priest serve the church, by fostering the development of a collective awareness that knows how to speak and to act according to the "We believe" (something far greater than the sum of the individual believers) and by promoting the type of cooperative action that we see in the pages of the New Testament. Such decision-making processes, where there is interdependence between the ministry of "one" and the participation of "all," are made possible precisely by the exercise of the *munus regendi ac pascendi* (LG 27; CD 16) of bishop and priest. Such processes produce, reproduce, and develop social values, interpret the people's shared history, and help people to perceive what it means "to be We."

However, it is important to address a number of limitations and resistances that prevent or impede the service of the "one" in processing information and defining criteria for judgment.[97] These include: (1) cognitive dissonance that leads to limited coherence between what is conceived and what is actually done; (2) an illusion of control that leads to overestimating one's own influence; (3) the projection of one's personal preferences onto the common path; (4) decisions taken regarding "extreme" phenomena that are considered the norm; and (5) stubborn adherence to the decisions made even when it becomes clear they are wrong. There is also the danger of surrounding oneself with "yes men" and not adequately heeding critical and dissenting voices or the voices of those, such as experts, who bring different perspectives. By slowing down shared discernment, limiting creativity, and restricting the possibility of profound change, these widespread attitudes and behaviors favor ineffective accommodation and prevent transformation. To improve the quality of decisions, such systemic blocks and distortions should be overcome by combining effectiveness and competence and by promoting integrated, collective decision-making processes. Rethinking *decision-making* is the "key organizational problem of our time,"[98] say the sociologists. This is true also for the church, particularly a church in reform.

A SYNODAL CHURCH

The rediscovery of synodality in the theology and magisterium of Pope Francis undoubtedly has its roots in the ecclesiological vision of Vatican II, which saw the church as the people of God, emphasizing subjectivity of the laity and a communal perspective. At the same time, we should not underestimate the influence that a widespread democratic, participatory sensibility has had in the reception of the Council and in the recovery of the "synodal" perspective. It is a sensibility that touches people's daily experience in many contexts throughout the world, from the field of politics to the contexts of work, education, and civic life.

The first years after the Council saw the publication of studies dedicated to the hoped-for democratization of the church; they called for a review of decision-making processes and the exercise of authority, and they recommended greater participation of the laity, such as would give a voice to all the baptized. In more recent times the studies have turned more directly to the theme of the synodal form of church. "Is a democratization *of* the church possible? Is the introduction of a democratic model *into* the church at least conceivable?" These are the questions posed by Giuseppe Alberigo at the beginning of the 1990s.[99] Certainly, it is not a matter of naively applying democratic organizational practices or models to the ecclesial context, but we would do well to ask whether democracy and synodality share common elements, similarities, and links that might allow for honest comparison and "mutual contamination"[100] between them.

The Catholic Church's resistance to affirming democracy is well known. For centuries the "ecclesial figure" has been shaped by the functional and symbolic assimilation of patriarchal, feudal, and monarchical forms of the *ancien régime*, in which the exercise of authority and hierarchy descends from above. We do not find Catholic thinkers among those who have promoted the cultural revolutions of modernity, including democracy.[101] There are many who consider democratization incompatible with the nature of the church, even though, historically, the exercise of ecclesial power has often assumed forms that were clearly marked by a "participatory-democratic logic." These include monastic chapters, the exercise of authority by the Dominicans, the election of religious superiors, and the holding of synods and councils.

A Useful Comparison

The comparison between democracy and synodality can be useful both for indicating the specific presuppositions of the synodal form of church and for rethinking the procedures and institutions that are needed to give credible concreteness to the church's synodal awareness. When we speak of "democracy," we are referring not only to a "political system" that exists in extremely diverse forms around the world, but also to the principle of order and the internal organization of a social group, to the procedures created to express the political will of the members, and to the widespread culture that supports and nourishes this whole complex arrangement. Striving for this "government of the people, by the people, and for the people," as Abraham Lincoln defined democracy (Gettysburg, 1863), allows us, first, to grasp the originality of the exercise of synodality in this social aggregation that is the church. Differences arise in any consideration of the degrees of participation, as well as about the ways decisions are made and are taken. *Lumen Gentium*, the Council's Dogmatic Constitution on the Church, reaffirmed the membership of all the baptized, declaring them all equal in dignity and co-responsible in the ecclesial mission. This basic recognition is always correlated with the affirmation of a constitutive pluralism of charisms and of asymmetrical relations in the ecclesial body that characterize the *forma ecclesiae*, including the pastoral ministry of certain ecclesial subjects (bishops, priests, and deacons).

The source of power is also different: in a democracy, it is the people; in the church, it is Christ who works through sacramental mediation, whether through baptism as the principle of membership for all or through ordination of ministers whose function is unique and irreplaceable in and for the "ecclesial We."

In the Catholic Church, authority is always simultaneously personal, collegial, and communal. Ordained ministers are constituted not by the delegation of power from the community (the people), but by ordination, a sacramental act that pertains to the mystery of faith as the *actio* of Christ and the church in the Holy Spirit. In the synodal church, defining *consensus* is not left to the vote of the majority, who are tasked with acting for the totality; rather *consensus* is sought through communicative interactions that, at least ideally, involve all the members who make up the church. The Catholic Church cannot develop its understanding of revelation and cannot make decisions according to the criteria of parliamentary democratic deliberation, that is, according to an exclusively quantitative type of majority/minority logic. Precisely for this reason, the ancient adage already mentioned, "*quod omnes tangit, ab omnibus tractari [et approbari] debet*," should be put into practice. At the same time, the criterion of seeking the *sanior pars*[102] and safeguarding the opinion of minorities should be observed. The church should not avoid being provoked by the uncomfortable prophetic voices that arise both within and without, because the Spirit works also in this way.

Democratic Processes

Even though the church is not a democracy, this does not mean that democratic procedures should be excluded in the exercise of synodality in all areas of the church's life (for example, appointment of bishops, pastoral councils and consultations, episcopal conferences, and lay movements). In this way, not only will the already codified participatory practices (cc. 127, 135ff., 208–223) be recognized and enhanced, but new practices deemed necessary by many but absent today will be implemented (such as publicity, transparency, and *accountability*).

The Reform of Structures

The organizational models that the church has adopted over the centuries have always been culturally defined and have included elements that are typical of the social organization of diverse places and times. The same can be said of the communicative-participative dynamics and deliberative processes by which the synodal form of church expresses itself. There are no synodal practices and institutions divorced from history, as can be seen from even a superficial comparison of the synods of the second and third centuries with the medieval councils, with Vatican II, or with the provincial councils and the post-conciliar diocesan synods. The ecclesial form received from the past was deeply marked by a feudal and monarchical *mens* that stressed the power of the "one-over-all." Such a form does not reflect the contemporary interpretative canon of social relations, which is democratic in its deepest core. The forms of participation and co-responsibility that characterize modern democracy help us to rediscover the logic of communion that, in the first centuries of Christianity, gave rise to participatory models that later disappeared (for example, the election of bishops). Such a logic conceives of authority in terms of relational power. Throughout history, synodality, as an essential dimension and *modus vivendi et operandi* of the church, has been realized in different ways. Today there is a growing demand to have this ordinary synodality embodied in every moment of ecclesial life, with the thorough involvement of laypeople.

Today's democratic experience, on the one hand, offers data that can help us assess the effectiveness of the contribution of all the baptized in synodal processes, as, for example, when questions are raised about the vote of the laity, which in all areas is always and exclusively consultative, or when a desire is expressed for greater involvement of women, for instance, by giving female auditors the vote in bishops' synods. Many questions are raised, therefore, by the democratic *mens*, that is, *participatory democracy*, the democratization of organizational systems, and the democratic practices familiar to citizens of Western nations: How should the church react to dissent? How is legitimate pluralism to be determined? How much freedom is allowed in theological research? How should public opinion be formed in the church, and what influence should it have on deliberations? And finally, what are the reasons for the persistence of a hierarchical mentality in the clergy? The question of synodality and the ways it is implemented is decisive for the church of the future; certain acquired democratic procedures can do much to help the church make its synodal will a reality.

On the other hand, Western parliamentary democracies are facing a crisis caused by a wide variety of factors: apathy, a weakening of political common sense, management and manipulation of public opinion, a top-heavy bureaucracy, and the distrust of many voters who are tempted by totalitarianism and fundamentalism that promise identity and security in the face of complexity. The church of today, as it rediscovers the meaning and value of synodality, can contribute to the development of a culture of encounter, dialogue, and co-responsibility. In so doing, it can not only uncover the root of the present problems, the limited forms of representation, but it can also rediscover the relationship between building consensus and the truth/good to be pursued.[103]

6

A People on the Move

"The path of synodality is the path that God expects from the church of the third millennium."[1] This decisive statement of Pope Francis in his Address Commemorating the Fiftieth Anniversary of the Institution of the Synod of Bishops (October 17, 2015) indicates the direction of the path of renewal for the church in the coming years. These words specify a *forma ecclesiae* that entails a conversion of mentality that will lead to a better understanding of ourselves, of the contribution of the other ecclesial members, of the constitutive principles of "doing church together," and of the urgent mission of the people of God. And such a conversion will, in turn, lead to a renewal of practices and structures at all levels and in all contexts of ecclesial life.

PRESUPPOSITIONS

The option for a "synodal church" represents a significant step in the process of receiving Vatican II.[2] Synodality is rooted in some of the Council's basic ecclesiological concepts, which were obscured after the 1990s: people of God, *sensus fidei*, local church. Nevertheless, the Council's vision of church, as presented in the second chapter of *Lumen Gentium*, has been rescued and given concrete synodal form in other valuable documents: the Apostolic Constitution *Episcopalis Communio*; the treatise of the International Theological Commission, "Synodality in the Life and Mission of the Church"; and the Preparatory Document of the Synod 2021–2023.

Lacking, in fact, were precise (institutionalized) ways to welcome the contributions made by the faithful's prophetic word and co-responsibility (except in pastoral councils). There was likewise a lack of ways to receive the contribution of the local churches at the level of the universal church, except through the voice of some bishops convened in regional and local synods. The Council documents, in the end, never fully define the link between episcopal collegiality, *communio ecclesiarum*, and the synodality of church as people of God.[3]

The vision of synodality that is now emerging from current practices, theological research, and magisterial documents defines not only the "ecclesiology of communion," to which we refer but also the participatory, communicative model that is required for the church to be truly a communion of all the faithful, thus helping to clarify what was stated in the Synod held in 1985, twenty years after Vatican II. The church has a communal essence and thrives from and in synodal forms.[4] These three aspects of church (historical-institutional subject, communion, and synodality) are kept closely interconnected, distinguishable but not separable, by the dynamic of communication of the faith.

At stake in the synodal form of church are the processes of institutionalization as the empirical plane of ecclesial life interacts with the mysterious, eschatological plane, thanks to the contributions of all the baptized. By the operation of the

Spirit, the "historical becoming" of the "ecclesial We" takes place through and in the communicative dynamics of faith and in faith that generates and regenerates the collective subject "church." Communion is at the level of essence, of the inner dynamics that distinguish the relationship with God and the relationship among people (as well as the relation among local churches), but synodality has to do with the empirically detectable processes of communication, discernment, decision-making, and collective implementation, all of which should be rooted in the participation of all the *christifideles* in the prophetic *munus* of Christ (see LG 12). Thus, the model of synodal church that is emerging today is based on the real involvement of everyone, since all the baptized are called to active participation.

This means creating inclusive spaces and structures that allow for speaking, dialogue, and listening, always with the awareness that the Spirit of the Lord can grant the church indications and suggestions through the voices of the smallest and youngest, as the Rule of Benedict states, or it can make demands of the church through the evolution of cultural values or even through the word and action of persecutors (see GS 44). At the heart of the ecclesial communion in synodal forms is a model of multidirectional asymmetrical communication: all the faithful are subjects of the word, and all are hearers of the Word of God and of the words of other believers, but ordained ministers have the specific function of attesting to the apostolic faith and of providing pastoral governance for the community. The synodal model in the Roman Catholic Church calls for the recognition of the specific contribution of those who have received a certain charism of truth, namely, the bishops (see DV 8, 10; LG 25, 37; CD 14). The bishops are the first custodians and promoters of a synodal church; they are the ones who orient the many voices of the ecclesial subjects, in all their rich variety, toward the *consensus*, thus ensuring a true "ecclesial polyphony."

The local church, as the *portio* of the people of God living in a given culture, is brought together by the Spirit around the Word of God and the Eucharist thanks to the ministry of the bishop, along with his priests and deacons (see CD 11). The local church, the "starting point" and primary focus of synodal renewal, "takes place" as "the response to the Gospel heard in one's own language in a specific human space (culture)," as this is expressed in the words of the believing subjects who co-constitute it.[5] Through interpersonal communication, the faithful share and reflect on their experiences, and this sharing constitutes the basis for the potential and effective "process of self-constitution" of the church, in the sense of its "taking place," "becoming," or "being fulfilled."[6] The church is built synodally; it is a collective subject that matures in faith and grows in its intra-ecclesial relations and mission because all the faithful are contributing to its ministerial synergy as they seek to understand and live the gospel. These are the two trajectories that mark the synodal form of church: the understanding of the gospel, which generates and regenerates the church; and the charismatic ministerial synergy that carries out the ecclesial mission.

As John Chrysostom taught, *"ekklesía gar systèmatos kai synódou estìn ónoma"*[7]: for him, the name of the church—that is, its recognized and proclaimed identity—is given in two related aspects, which form a kind of hendiadys. The first term has to do with agreeing or being together; the second, with walking together, thus adding a dynamic element. Both Greek terms have the prefix *"syn-,"* which indicates a constitutive relation. All this happens simultaneously on several levels, from that of the local churches to that of the universal church: it involves the contribution of individual ecclesial subjects at the local level, along with the ministry proper to the bishop. More broadly, it happens in the relations between local churches at the regional and universal levels, and it happens through the mediation of the bishops who are members of the college, under and with the bishop of Rome. In all cases, the fulcrum is the promotion of multidirectional, networked communicational dynamics that potentially involve everyone, with their diverse charisms and ministries and in the great variety of traits that characterize the local churches.

STRUCTURAL REFORM

"There can be no church life, no expression of ecclesial being, except as a synodal event."[8] As we have seen, this awareness must be translated into the free and courageous reconfiguration of the church's ministry and into an intelligent transformation of the structures and organization of the community life of the local churches. In the past, however, the Christian community has undergone real reforms, reforms in which a new vision of church shaped the collective consciousness and substantial changes were pursued for the sake of greater fidelity to the gospel. Sometimes also—precisely in synodal contexts—a common language or conduct was sought in the face of abuses, erroneous theological positions, divisions, or schisms.

Every reform is marked by a precise intentionality and is guided by a vision of the ideal church that calls for the commitment of all. Vatican II was a council of reform, as was the Council of Trent. This was the declared intention of both Popes John XXIII and Paul VI, and the constitutions, decrees, and declarations of Vatican II are all oriented toward reform. On the one hand, the reception of the Council shows that certain reforms (as in the liturgy) have already taken place; on the other, there is evident resistance to further necessary changes, accompanied by stagnation and a desire to return to the past. Thanks to the magisterial hermeneutics of many bishops in recent decades and, specifically, of Pope Francis, the ecclesiology of Vatican II has taken on a renewed vigor and has motivated commitment to the prospect of synodal reform. This willingness requires more than a simple change of mentality, pastoral conversion, and the modification of certain styles of behavior. It must also entail serious reforms that involve transforming structures, especially as regards reconceiving ordained ministry; recognizing the subjectivity of women; inculturating the church (and not only the faith); remodeling ecclesial power and authority; improving the ways of exercising governance; and making the procedures for deliberation more inclusive. The proposals made here are meant as suggestions, so that the synodal harmonization of the "one," the "some," and the "all" can be realized first of all in the local churches and so that both trajectories, that of the *systematos* and that of the *synodos* can be realized concretely in the life of dioceses and parishes.

The transformation of the church from a synodal perspective is necessary so that the faithful accept the vision of the church as the people of God (see LG 9, 12); so that they experience catholicity fully as unity in differences, in a church that has become worldwide (see LG 13; AG); so that they fulfill their ecumenical vocation (see LG 14–15) to be a sign and instrument of an inclusive communion (see LG 1) in today's globalized, democratic world; and so that they assess critically any institution that thinks of itself as an immutable entity or that governs on the basis of an autocratic, bureaucratic, monarchical, kyriarchical, exclusively male principle of authority. This reform from a synodal perspective comes at a dramatic time, when thousands of cases of sex abuse and abuse of conscience, power, and gender committed by clergy or lay pastoral workers have been discovered.

The scandals have brought to light the inadequacy of an ecclesial system in which those in authority are answerable only to those who occupy an upper rung in the hierarchy; such a system lacks transparency and promotes a culture of silence, doggedly defending the institution and its men even when very serious shortcomings come to light. It is now clear that significant change is needed in the communications model that makes us church, and that such change will come about only through the adoption of a dialogical style that promotes convergence on essential matters and a progressively maturing consensus. Space must be allowed for the criticism and the dissonant opinions of those who have other ways of seeing, acting, and judging reality.

Finally, structural change requires, on the one hand, an ecclesiology that is more attentive to pneumatology and more capable of rethinking the themes of tradition, apostolicity, and catholicity from a dynamic perspective; on the other hand, it must pursue more systematic collaboration with sociology, political science, social pedagogy, and the human sciences generally. Without these contributions, ecclesiology cannot address the sensitive issue of leadership, nor can it define new communicational and organizational dynamics.

TRANSFORMATIONAL LEADERSHIP

How is it possible to promote reform with a synodal logic? Who can lead the church along this path and make clear the theological, pastoral, and cultural reasons that make reform necessary and urgent? Certainly, in our post-Tridentine church, the authority and the power to decide and promote reform lie fundamentally with the pope, the bishops, and the clergy. Pope Francis's call for synodal reform has opened a path on which laypeople are encouraged to point out problems, present new ecclesial visions, and propose diverse experiences of existence and faith. On this path, the laity find a space in which they are finally heard and where they feel co-responsible for the reform of the church.

Synodality is already the form of church projected in Vatican II and developed in the postconciliar reception, but persistent promotion of synodal institutes and occasions is necessary so that everyone can contribute to the projects of reform. To understand how this process can take place, we can go back to the Acts of the Apostles, which narrates an initial synodal experience, even prior to the "assembly in Jerusalem" (Acts 15). In Acts 6:1–7, we find all the key elements of a synodal dynamic: cultural differences, nagging conflicts, stages of discernment, and reconciling dialogue between those with pastoral responsibility and the concerned members to the community. In the very first verse, Luke presents the context as one of growth and development ("the disciples were increasing in number"), but the Christians were facing a new situation, and a crisis was looming because of cultural diversity. All the members of the Jerusalem community were Jewish Christians, but some were Greek-speaking (the "Hellenists") while others were Aramaic-speaking. The two groups had different spiritual attitudes (the former more open, the latter more conservative), attended different synagogues, and perhaps celebrated somewhat different liturgies since the Hellenists used the Greek translation of the scriptures (the Septuagint) while the others used the Hebrew text. Although both groups shared the common identity of belonging to Israel and having faith in Christ, there were differences in the ways they conceived and lived the Christian ecclesial experience, and these differences could be seen in the liturgy, in the formulations of faith, and in the organization of community life.

As was to be expected, the differences created tension, but for a time the tension was not perceived and discussed. The conflict first surfaced in a practical matter: part of the community was being neglected in the provision of community services. A situation of injustice had been created regarding the Hellenist widows, who were the weakest social subjects since they lacked the support of their husbands and could not count on the help of an extended family because they came from other regions. The Hellenist Jews expressed their discontent with the situation with quiet but unmistakable murmuring (in Greek *goggusmos*, the term used to indicate the Israelites' murmuring during the Exodus). The problem in the community was at the level of relationships, and it revealed infidelity to the logic of the gospel. Moreover, it had indirect repercussions beyond the community because the management of economic affairs was not being conducted according to the justice of the Gospel (see Acts 2:42–46; "there was not a needy person among them," Acts 4:34). The community was no longer a sign of the coming of the kingdom of God and the good news of the gospel, the revelation that had created great interest and sympathy among the people.

When the community was faced with this problem, a synodal dynamic was set in motion, a dynamic that involved everyone even though their responsibilities were different. The Twelve convened the assembly of all the faithful so that everyone was involved in the community discernment. The Twelve analyzed the reality with extreme lucidity, and they tackled the problem by going to the root cause, the tension between the two groups, but they did so thoughtfully, without being shocked by the existing tension, without limiting themselves to the "symptoms" (the neglected widows), and without delaying decisions in a way that would exacerbate the tension. After identifying the needs of the community entrusted to them, they not only attended to the concrete needs but also dealt with the underlying problem. They did not appeal to spiritual principles and call people to prayer without first elaborating a sensible operational choice.

The Twelve understood that the problem did not concern just a few people (the "some") whose essential needs were not being recognized; it involved the whole community. The embryonic organization had until then seen the Twelve as its first leaders, having exclusive central roles, but the new situation required a different type of church organization. The Twelve were willing to change the "figure of the church" and to rethink ecclesial roles and powers, giving up some functions that they had been managing until then. Though the Twelve had the power to convene and to lay down the norms necessary for true community life, they did not come to a decision on their own—and then communicate it to the community with the expectation that all would passively receive it. Rather, they promoted a synodal dynamic so that the members would understand that they had different roles to play but that they all were responsible for the future. After explaining the situation, using a declaration of principle and a motivating argument, the Twelve created a new ministerial form that responded to the need, thus reshaping the ecclesial institution and its organization. The word *diakonia* occurs three times in the passage, indicating the service provided to the widows, the function proper to the Twelve (*diakonia* of the Word), and the function proper to the Seven (*diakonia* of the tables). What the Twelve had administered directly until then was now entrusted to others who formed a second "collective ministerial college": in other words, pastoral functions and tasks were differentiated, and roles were separated by engaging other members of the church. Thus, a synergistic dynamic was activated that had not existed before; it was a synodal dynamic that allowed for reform of ecclesial relations and actions.

The leadership of the Twelve was transformative: they understood the specificity of their ministry and were willing to redefine their identity, but they insisted on involving the community in a way that demonstrated their freedom from desire of position and possessions. After indicating the criteria, the Twelve allowed the community to decide who were the most suitable persons, and the community was "pleased" with this way of proceeding, the text says. After engaging in discernment, the community chose seven persons whose Greek names indicate that they came from the part of the community that was experiencing the situation of injustice and weakness. The last one, Nicholas, was said to be a proselyte, that is, a pagan convert who was not Jewish by birth. We can imagine that the community made their selection after debating the proposal of the Twelve and considering the candidates who met the criteria indicated. There was no casting of lots, as happened in the case of Matthias, but rather a "democratic-participatory" dynamic in which arguments were presented and decisions were made.

Truly transformative leadership knows how to open up to new leaders who, as in this case, must be honest and impartial and held in irreproachable esteem among the faithful. They should be full of spiritual wisdom because as part of the community leadership they will have to speak publicly and be capable of right discernment. The figure of these new pastoral leaders in the community was created by the Twelve, but it was inspired by the existing social organization known as the "Seven," a collective body that oversaw the Jewish communities in the diaspora. After the community indicated its wishes, the Twelve, by virtue of the ministry they held, performed a liturgical gesture of mandate and empowerment. The gesture was taken from the Jewish tradition, but it was redefined; according to Jewish custom, the laying on of hands was used to establish a leader, to consecrate the Levites, and to ordain rabbis and members of the Sanhedrin. The conclusion of the narrative, in Acts 6:7, shows that the crisis, which could have torn the community apart, was transformed into a blessing: the number of believers grew "greatly" after that. This adverb— absent in verse 1—speaks of the positive resolution of a crisis that could have split or weakened the nascent Christian community.

A SYNODAL SPIRITUALITY

Reform in a synodal key requires us to assume the spiritual attitude of "displacement": we need to relinquish our unquestioned assumptions and our consolidated habits and traditions so as to view ourselves and our reality with other eyes. We need to welcome the possibility given to us of living in other places, following other paths, discovering other opportunities. The "ecclesial We" matures in synodal fashion, through dialogue, conversation, discussion, discernment in common, and the reconciliation of differing opinions that at first sight appear irreconcilable. Living synodally means going beyond the routines that give security; it means being open to research, to change, and to the not-yet of the promise of God's kingdom. Those who live this time of the church in faith and hope are not concerned with self-affirmation but are passionate about the "common end." They do not sacralize the ecclesial structures received from the past because they know that the constitutive essence will be preserved through all the necessary change of figures, forms, and practices. "Every renewal of the Church is essentially grounded in an increase of fidelity to her own calling....Christ summons the Church to continual reformation as she sojourns here on earth. The Church is always in need of this" (UR 6).

Notes

INTRODUCTION

1. R. Luciani, *Synodality: A New Way of Proceeding in the Church* (New York / Mahwah, NJ: Paulist Press, 2022).

2. In the Italian and Spanish editions of the book, the two contributions by Rafael Luciani and Serena Noceti are collected in one volume. Italian edition: *Sinodalmente. Forma e riforma di una chiesa sinodale* (Florence: Nerbini, 2022); the Spanish edition will be published in 2023. In this American edition, the first two chapters of this volume are original.

3. R. Barthes, *Frammenti di un discorso amoroso* (Turin: Einaudi, 1979), 5.

CHAPTER 1

1. This contribution reproduces, expanding on some passages, an article published in Italian under the title "La sinodalità dimensione della chiesa," *Orientamenti pastorali* 69 (2021) xii, 32–47.

2. See R. Luciani and M.T. Compte, eds., *En camino hacia una iglesia sinodal. De Pablo VI a Francisco* (Madrid: PPC, 2020); R. Luciani and M.P. Silveira, eds., *La sinodalidad en la vita de la Iglesia: Reflexiones para contribuir a la reforma eclesial* (Madrid: San Pablo, 2020); D. Vitali,

Un popolo in cammino verso Dio: La sinodalità in Evangelii gaudium (Milan: S. Paolo, 2018). See also L. Baldisseri, ed., *A cinquant'anni dalla Apostolica Sollicitudo: Il Sinodo dei vescovi al servizio di una chiesa sinodale* (Vatican City, LEV, 2016); R. Repole, "Quale sinodalità per quale Chiesa: A bibliographical review of a theme born on the quiet and now central to Francis' magisterium," *Il Regno Attualità* 14 (2018): 411–15; G. Calabrese, *Ecclesiologia sinodale* (Bologna: EDB, 2021).

3. For an introductory, overall view, see G. Canobbio, "Sulla sinodalità," *Teologia* 41 (2016): 249–73; A. Melloni and S. Scatena, eds., *Synod and Synodality* (Münster: LIT, 2005), Acts of a conference held in Bruges in 2003; G. Alberigo, *Conciliar Church: Identity and Meaning of Conciliarism* (Rome: Paideia, 1981); E. Corecco, "Sinodalità," in *Nuovo Dizionario di Teologia* (Milan: Paoline, 2000), 1466–1495; Corecco, "Ontology of Synodality," in *Pastor bonus in populo*, ed. A. Autiero and O. Carena (Rome: Città Nuova, 1990), 303–29. An extensive bibliography, compiled by A. Dal Pozzolo and S. Segoloni, can be found in R. Battocchio and L. Tonello, eds., *Sinodalità: Dimensione della Chiesa, pratiche nella chiesa* (Padua: EMP, 2020), 527–65.

4. See C.M. Bravi, *Il Sinodo dei vescovi, istituzione, fini e natura* (Rome: PUG, 1995); A. Indelicato, *Il Sinodo dei Vescovi: La collegialità sospesa (1965–1985)* (Bologna: Il Mulino, 2008).

5. See A. Join-Lambert, ed., *Synodes diocésains, "parasynodes" et conciles particuliers dans l'Église catholique depuis le Concile Vatican II*, Liste, bibliographie, resources (Louvain LN and Paris, Quebec: Cahiers Internationaux de teologie pratique, 2016); H.M. Legrand, "Synodes et conseils de l'après-concile," *Nouvelle Revue Théologique* 98 (1976): 193–216.

6. G. Hammann, "'Synode' et 'Synodalite.' Histoire et enjeux d'un concept ecclésiologique," *Positions Luthériennes* 46 (1998): 131–55.

7. H.M. Legrand, "Collégialité des évêques et communion des églises dans la réception de Vatican II," *Revue des Sciences Philosophiques et Théologiques* 75 (1991): 545–68; Legrand, "La synodalità, dimensione inerente alla vita ecclesiale. Fondamenti e attualità," *Vivens Homo*

16 (2005): 7–42; Legrand, "Lo sviluppo di chiese-soggetto: un'istanza del Vaticano II. Theological foundations and institutional reflections," *Cristianesimo nella Storia 2.* (1981): 129–64; G. Routhier, "La synodalité de l'Eglise locale," *Studia canonica* 26 (1992): 111–61; J. M. R. Tillard, *Chiesa di chiese. L'ecclesiologia di comunione* (Brescia:, Queriniana, 1989). See also S. Dianich, "Sinodalità," in *Teologia* (Cinisello Balsamo: San Paolo, 2002): 1522–31. See also the International Colloquia of Salamanca: H.M. Legrand, J. Manzanares, and A. Garcia y Garcia, eds., *Chiese locali e cattolicità* (Bologna: EDB, 1994); H. Legrand, J. Manzanares, and A. Garcia y Garcia, eds., *Reconciliation and Communion among the Churches. Acts of the International Colloquium of Salamanca, 8–14 April, 1996* (Bologna: EDB, 1998).

   8. R. Battocchio and S. Noceti, eds., *Chiesa e sinodalità. Consciousness, forms, processes* (Milan: Glossa,2007). See G. Ancona, ed., Dossier *Chiesa e sinodalità*, Velar, Gorla BG 2005, which collects the texts of the preparatory pre-congresses.

   9. Many of the contributions of the Seminar of Studies on Church Reform held at *Civiltà Cattolica* in 2015 focus on the synodal form of church; see A. Spadaro and C.M. Galli, eds., *La Riforma e le Riforme nella Chiesa* (Brescia: Queriniana, 2016).

   10. See R. Luciani and S. Noceti, "Imparare un ecclesialità sinodale," *Attualità* 66 (2021): viii, 257–64.

   11. Francis, "Address at the Ceremony Commemorating the 50th Anniversary of the Institution of the Synod of Bishops," October 17, 2015, www.vatican.va/.

   12. Francis, *Episcopalis communio* (September 15, 2018), www.vatican.va/.

   13. Francis, "Address at the Ceremony Commemorating the 50th Anniversary of the Institution of the Synod of Bishops."

   14. See International Theological Commission, "Synodality in the Life and Mission of the Church" (March 2, 2018), www.vatican.va/. See P. Coda and R. Repole, eds., *La sinodalità nella vita e nella missione della chiesa* (Bologna: EDB, 2019).

15. See S. Noceti, "Commentary on *Christus Dominus*," in *Commentary on the Documents of Vatican II*, ed. S. Noceti and R. Repole, vol. 4 (Bologna: EDB, 2017).

16. G. Ruggieri, "I sinodi tra storia e teologia," in *Chiesa e Sinodalità*, ed. R. Battocchio and S. Noceti, 129–61, at 160.

17. I take up here some ecclesiological reflections on synodality that I have developed more extensively in "Synodality: A Reflection in Ecclesiological Key," in *La sinodalità al tempo di papa Francesco*, ed. N. Salato (Bologna: EDB, 2020), 153–69; "Forma sinodale di chiesa," in *Forma e forme della chiesa: Per una chiesa estroversa*, ed. A. Clemenzia (Florence: Nerbini, 2020), 61–72.

18. See S. Dianich, "Attraversati dalla storia," *Attualità* 64 (2019): 493–505; G. Routhier, "Il Rinnovamento della vita sinodale nelle chiese locali," in *La riforma e le riforme nella chiesa*, ed. A. Spadaro and C.M. Galli (Brescia: Queriniana, 2016), 233–47; A. Borras, "Ecclesial Synodality, Participatory Processes and Decision-Making Modes: Il punto di vista di un canonista," in *La riforma e le riforme nella chiesa*, ed. A. Spadaro and C.M. Galli, 207–32.

19. See C. Duquoc, "The People of God as an Active Subject of Faith in the Church," *Concilium* 21 (1985): 4, 100–111.

20. John Chrysostom, *Ex. in Psalm.* 149,2: *PG* 55,493.

21. See H. Vorgrimler, "Dal '*sensus fidei*' al '*consensus fidelium*'," *Concilium* 21 (1985): 489–500.

22. D. Vitali, "Universitas fidelium in credendo falli nequit (LG 12): Il sensus fidelium al Concilio Vaticano II," *Gregorianum* 86 (2005): 607–28; Vitali., "La circolarità tra sensus fidei e magistero come criterio per l'esercizio della sinodalità nella chiesa," in *La riforma e le riforme nella chiesa*, ed. Spadaro and Galli; S. Noceti, "*Sensus fidelium*: An Ecclesiological Reflection, in *La morale ecclesiale tra sensus fidelium e magistero*, ed. A. Rovello (Assisi: Cittadella, 2016), 37–59.

23. Y.M. Congar, "Quod omnes tangit, ab omnibus tractari et approbari debet," *Revue historique de droit français et étranger* 36 (1958): 210–59. See International Theological Commission, "Synodality," 65.

Notes

24. International Theological Commission, "Synodality," 64. 106; see also Legrand, *Synodality as an Inherent Dimension*, 12–19.

25. International Theological Commission, "Synodality," 74.

26. International Theological Commission, "Synodality," 3, 43, 67, 22, 107.

27. See R. Repole, *Come stelle in terra: La Chiesa nell'epoca della secolarizzazione* (Assisi: Cittadella, 2012).

28. See C. Schickendantz, "Elitismo y clericalismo: La conversión sinodal y la crisis de los abusos," in *Reforma de estructuras y conversion de mentalidades. Retos y desafíos para una iglesia sinodal*, ed. R. Luciani and C. Schickendantz (Madrid: Khaf, 2020), 231–58; L. de Kerimel, *En finir avec le cléricalisme* (Paris: Seuil, 2020).

29. S. Noceti, "What Structures for a Church in Reform?," *Concilium* 54 (2018): 652–68.

30. B. Hinze, "Can We Find a Way Together? The Challenge of Synodality in a Wounded and Wounding Church," *Irish Theological Quarterly* 85 (2020): 215.

31. International Theological Commission, "Synodality," 73; see also A. De Almeida, "Laicos y laicas en la práctica de la sinodalidad," in *La sinodalidad en la vida de la Iglesia: Reflexiones para contribuir a la reforma eclesial*, ed. R. Luciani and M.P. Silveira, 243–76; L. Clavell, "Il primo livello di sinodalità e l'ascolto della voce dei fedeli laici," in *A cinquant'anni dall'Apostolica sollicitudo: il *Sinodo dei Vescovi al servizio di una Chiesa sinodale*, ed. L. Baldisseri (Vatican City: LEV, 2016), 299–306.

32. I have explored this topic in "Laity and Synodality: A Necessary Word," in *Synodality in the Life and Mission of the Church*, ed. P. Coda and R. Repole, 93–105, and in "On the Pontificate of Pope Francis: The Keys to Reform—Starting with Leadership," *Attualità* 64 (2019): 249–52.

33. See A. Borras, "Ecclesial Synodality, Participatory Processes and Decision-Making: Il punto di vista di un canonista," in *La riforma e le riforme nella chiesa*, ed. A. Spadaro and C.M. Galli, 207–32; S. Segoloni, "Chiesa e sinodalità: indagine sulla struttura ecclesiale

a partire dal Vaticano II," *Convivium Assisiense* 14 (2012): 55–77; 15 (2013): 107–44; my proposal in this direction in "Elaborare Decisioni nella Chiesa. An Ecclesiological Reflection" (Clergy Course, October 22, 2019), 237–54.

34. International Theological Commission, "Synodality," 68, 100.

35. B. Jessop, *Social Order, Reform and Revolution. A Power, Exchange, and Institutionalization Perspective* (New York: Herder & Herder, 1972), 54.

36. C. Schickendantz, "Church Reform Also in Structures," *The Current Kingdom* 61 (2016): 4, 77ff.

CHAPTER 2

1. See D. Vitali, "Una Chiesa di Popolo: il sensus fidei come principio dell'evangelizzazione," in Evangelii gaudium: *il testo ci interroga*, ed. H.M. Yáñez (Rome: Gregorian & Biblical Press, 2014), 53–66.

2. See Pontifical Council for Social Communications, *Communio et Progressio* (1971), 25, 32, 116, 117 (on public opinion); Congregation for the Doctrine of the Faith, *Mysterium Ecclesiae* (1973), 2; Congregation for the Doctrine of the Faith, *Christian Freedom and Liberation* (1986), 98; Congregation for the Doctrine of the Faith, *Donum Veritatis* (1990), 35 ("the opinions of the faithful cannot be identified with the *sensus fidei*"); *Catechism of the Catholic Church*, 91–93, 785, 889. There are no references to the *sensus fidei* in the Code of Canon Law, apart from an allusion in c. 750 §1. See D. Burghardt, *Institution Glaubenssinn. Die Bedeutung des sensus fidei im kirchlichen Verfassungsrecht und für die Interpretation kanonischer Gesetze* (Paderborn: Bonifatius, 2000).

3. For an initial introduction to the debate on the *sensus fidei/ fidelium*, see D. Vitali, Sensus fidelium. *Una funzione ecclesiale di intelligenza della fede* (Brescia: Morcelliana, 1993); Z. Alszeghy, "Il senso della fede e lo sviluppo dogmatico," in *Il Vaticano II. Bilancio e prospettive venticinque anni dopo*, ed. R. Latourelle, vol. I (Assisi: Cittadella,

Notes

1987), 136–51; D.J. Finucane, Sensus fidelium. *The Use of a Concept in the Post-Vatican Era* (San Francisco: 1996); O. Rush, *The Eyes of Faith. The Sense of the Faithful and the Church's Reception of Revelation* (Washington, DC: Catholic University of America Press, 2009); J. Kerkhofs, "Le peuple de Dieu est-il infaillible? L'importance du 'sensus fidelium' dans l'église post-conciliaire," *Freiburger Zeitschrift* 35 (1988): 3–19; P.J. Hartin, "*Sensus Fidelium*: A Roman Catholic Reflection on Its Significance for Ecumenical Thought," *Journal of Ecumenical Studies* 28 (1991): 74–87; J. Burkhard, "*Sensus fidei*: Meaning, Role and Future of a Teaching of Vatican II," *Louvain Studies* 17 (1992): 18–34. See J. J. Burkhard, "*Sensus fidei*: Recent Theological Reflection (1990–2001)," *Heythrop Journal* 47 (2006): 38–54.

4. International Theological Commission, "The *sensus fidei* in the Life of the Church" (2014).

5. The lemma "*sensus*" is polysemic: it ranges from "meaning," to immediate intuition, to feeling/senses; it combines a passive receptive aspect with a dimension of unveiling activity. This makes it difficult to understand LG 12. It is useful to recall locutions similar to *sensus fidei/sensus fidelium* that appear in the council documents: *sensus fidei* (LG 12; PO 9); *sensus christianus fidelium* (GS 52); *sensus christianus* (GS 62); *sensus religiosus* (NAe 2; DH 4; GS 59), *sensus Dei* (DV 15; GS 7); *sensus Christi et ecclesiae* (AG 19). See O. Rush, "*Sensus Fidei*: Faith 'Making Sense' of Revelation," *Theological Studies* 62 (2001): 231–61; Ch. Ohly, "*Sensus fidei fidelium*. Zur Einordnung des Glaubenssinnes aller Gläubigen in die Communio-Struktur der Kirche im geschichtlichen Spiegel dogmatisch-kanonistischer Erkenntnisse und der Aussagen des II. Vaticanum," St. Ottilien (1999): 273–82.

6. Far from being a meta-application of the texts, of the letter of the documents, it is an overall transformative process in which the entire people of God is the protagonist, welcoming the conciliar event and what has been defined in the documents and shaping its life on the basis of what has been lived and indicated. See Y.M. Congar, "La réception comme rèalité ecclesiologique," *Revue des Sciences Philosophiques et Théologiques* 56 (1972): 369–403; G. Routhier, *Il Concilio Vaticano II:*

Recezione ed ermeneutica (Milan: Vita e Pensiero, 2006); Ch. Theobald, *La recezione del Vaticano II*, "Part I. Tornare alla fonte" (Bologna: EDB, 2011), 389–541.

7. I have explored this topic in S. Noceti, "*Sensus fidelium* and the Ecclesial Dynamics," in *Authentic Voices–Discerning Hearts: New Resources for the Church on Marriage and Family*, ed. Th. Knieps-Port Le Roy and A. Brenninkmeijer-Werhahn (Zürich: LIT Verlag, 2016), 170–83; Noceti, "*Sensus fidelium*. An Ecclesiological Reflection," in *La morale ecclesiale tra sensus fidelium e magistero*, ed. A. Rovello (Assisi: Cittadella, 2016), 37–59.

8. M. Cano, *De locis theologicis*, IV, 2 concl. 1 and 2; R. Bellarmino, *De controversiis*, liber III; J.A. Möhler, *L'unità nella chiesa. Il principio del cattolicesimo nello spirito dei Padri della chiesa dei primi tre secoli* (Rome: Città Nuova, 1969 [orig. 1825]; J.H. Newman, *Sulla consultazione dei fedeli in materia di dottrina* (Brescia: Morcelliana, 1991 [orig. *On Consulting the Faithful in Matters of Doctrine,*1832]; see R.W. Schmucker, *Sensus fidei: Der Glaubenssinn in seiner vorkonziliaren Entwicklungsgeschichte und in den Dokumenten des Zweiten Vatikanischen Konzils* (Regensburg: Roderer Verlag, 1998).

9. See Pius IX, *Ineffabilis Deus*, in Acta Pii IX 1/597–616; Pius XII, Dogmatic Constitution *Munificentissimus Deus* (1.12.1950), no. 36: *AAS* 42 (1950): 753–73.

10. On *Lumen gentium* 12 and the history of its drafting, see the contribution of D. Vitali, "*Lumen gentium,*" in *Commentary on the Documents of Vatican II*, ed. S. Noceti and R. Repole (Bologna: EDB, 2015), 176–185; Ch. Ohly, *Sensus fidei fidelium. Zur Einordnung des Glaubenssinnes aller Gläubigen in die Communio-Struktur der Kirche im geschichtlichen Spiegel dogmatisch-kanonistischer Erkenntnisse und der Aussagen des II. Vaticanum* (Oberbayern: St. Ottilien, 1999), 173–72; J. Sancho, *Infalibilidad del Pueblo de Dios: sensus fidei e infalibilidad orgánica de la Iglesia en la Lumen Gentium* (Pamplona, 1979); D. Vitali, "Universitas fidelium in credendo falli equità" (LG 12). "The sensus fidelium at the Second Vatican Council," *Gregorianum* 86 (2005): 607–28; B. Van Leeuwen, "La partecipazione comune del popolo di Dio all'ufficio

propetico di Cristo," in *La Chiesa del Vaticano II. Studi e commenti intorno alla Costituzione dommatica "Lumen gentium,"* ed. G. Baraúna (Florence: Vallecchi, 1965), 465–90. The text of LG 12 takes up in large part the textus prior, at § 24, which presented the prophetic *munus* of the laity: the theme was already present in the *Schema preparatorio*, it remains in the *Schema Philips* but refers only to the laity. After Cardinal Suenens' request for a chapter dedicated to the people of God, the *sensus fidei* is presented as qualifying the subjectivity of all the baptized and of the entire messianic people, decisively going beyond the idea of a passive *infallibilitas* for the faithful.

11. See the replacement of "*ecclesia tota*" in the textus prior by "*universitas fidelium.*"

12. See D. Vitali, "The Totality of the Faithful cannot be mistaken in believing (LG 12): The *sensus fidelium* as the Voice of Tradition," *Urbaniana University Journal* 66 (2013): 37–70.

13. L. Sartori, "Il '*sensus fidelium*' del popolo di Dio e il concorso dei laici nelle determininazioni docrinali," *Studi Ecumenici* 6 (1988): 33–57; Chr. Duquoc, "Il popolo di Dio, soggettivo attivo della fede nella chiesa," *Concilium* 21 (1985): 574–85; G. Albano, *Il sensus fidelium: la partecipazione del Popolo di Dio alla funzione propetica di* Cristo (Naples: Pontificia Facoltà teologica dell'Italia meridionale, 2008).

14. Unfinished, in some respects, given its specific eschatological opening, as stated in DV 8.

15. R. Guardini, *La vita della fede* (Brescia: Morcelliana, 2008), 96 [orig. 1965].

16. I develop my reflections on a synodal church bearing in mind the sociological studies of P.L. Berger and Th. Luckmann, *La realtà come costruzione sociale* (Bologna: Il Mulino, 1969 [orig. 1966]); T. Parsons, *Il sistema sociale* (Milan: Comunità, 1965 [orig. 1951]); J. Habermas, *Teoria dell'agire comunicativo* (Bologna: Il Mulino, 1987–88 [orig. *The Theory of Communicative Action*, 1981]).

17. Vincent of Lerins, *Commonitorium*, 2, in PL 50, 640.

18. See P. Scharr, *Consensus fidelium. Unfehlbarkeit der Kirche aus der Perspektive einer Konsensustheorie der Wahrheit* (Würzburg: Echter,

1992); H. Wagner, "Glaubenssinn, Glaubenszustimmung, Glauben-konsensus," *Theologie und Glaube* 69 (1979): 263–71; R. Brosse, "*Consensus fidelium*: un dialogue? Réflexions herméneutiques sur la théologie fondamentale et l'ecclésiologie," *Revue Théologique de Louvain* 29 (1998): 331–44.

19. See H. Vorgrimler, Dal "'sensus fidei' al 'consensus fidelium,'" *Concilium* 21 (1985): 489–500.

20. J.H. Newman, *On Consulting the Faithful in Matters of Doctrine* (Brescia: Morcelliana, 1991 [orig. 1832]).

21. D. Vitali, "Magisterium and *Sensus fidelium*," *Revista Catalana de Teología* 39 (2014): 97–128; B. Sesboüé, *Le magistère à l'épreuve. Autorité, vérité et liberté dans l'Église* (Paris: Desclée de Brouwer, 2001).

22. G. Mucci, "Infallibilità della chiesa, magistero e autorità docrinale dei fedeli," *La Civiltà Cattolica* 139, no. 1 (1988): 431–42; E. Castelli, ed., *L'infallibilità. L'aspetto filosofico e teologico* (Rome: Istituto di studi filosofici, 1970); J.F. Chiron, *L'infaillibilité et son objet. L'autorité du magistère infaillible de l'église s'étend-elle aux vérités non révélées?* (Paris: Editions du Cerf, 1999).

23. D. Wiederkehr, ed., *Der Glaubenssinn des Gottesvolkes-Konkurrent oder Partner des Lehramts?* (Freiburg: Herder, 1994).

24. W. Kasper, *Die Lehre von der Tradition in der Römischen Schule*, quoted by H. Fries, "C'è un magistero dei fedeli," *Concilium* 17 (1985): 598.

25. Y.M. Congar, "An Attempt at a Catholic Synthesis," *Concilium* 17 (1981): 1318.

26. H. Legrand, "Reception, *sensus fidelium*, and Synodal Life: An Effort at Articulation," in *Reception and Communion among Churches*, ed. H. Legrand and J. Manzanares and Garcia y Garcia (Washington, DC: Catholic University of America, 1997), 405–31.

27. Congregation for the Doctrine of the Faith, "Instruction on Christian Freedom and Liberation," March 22, 1986, 98, www.vatican.va.

Notes

CHAPTER 3

1. We are thinking of the greater involvement of the laity, as happened in the two Synods on the Family, with the invitation to respond to the two preparatory questionnaires, and in the Synod on Young People, with an *ad hoc* questionnaire and a preassembly with about three hundred young people, or the strong involvement of the local churches in the Synod for Amazonia (87,000 people). See R. Luciani, "Reforma, conversión pastoral y sinodalidad. Un nuevo modo eclesial de proceder," in *En camino hacia una iglesia sinodal. De Pablo VI a Francisco*, ed. R. Luciani and M.T. Compte (Madrid: PPC, 2020), 165–88; R. Luciani and M.P. Silveira, ed., *La sinodalidad en la vita de la Iglesia. Reflexiones para contribuir a la reforma eclesial* (Madrid: San Pablo, 2020).

2. Francis, "Address on the occasion of the commemoration of the 50th anniversary of the establishment of the Synod of Bishops," October 17, 2015, www.vatican.va.

3. Francis, Apostolic Constitution *Episcopalis communio*, September 15, 2018, www.vatican.va; see M. Visioli, *Novelties for the Synod of Bishops: The Apostolic Constitution* Episcopalis communio, in *Synodality. Dimensione della Chiesa, pratiche nella chiesa*, ed. R. Battocchio and L. Tonello (Padua: EMP, 2020), 323–42.

4. Synod 2021–23, Preparatory Document and Vademecum.

5. G. Routhier, "The Renewal of Synodal Life in the Local Churches," in *La riforma e le riforme nella chiesa*, ed. A. Spadaro and C.M. Galli (Brescia: Queriniana, 2016), 233–47.

6. I take this idea from M. Bakhtin, *Problems of Dostoevsky's Poetics* (Minneapolis: University of Minnesota Press, 1984 [orig. 1929]), which applies it to the knowledge of truth: a single person alone cannot reach it because truth, to be told, needs a multiplicity of subjects interacting with each other. Conversation is a system of collective understanding. S. Noceti, "In comunicazione generativa: conversazione, consensus,

conspiratio," in *Sinodalità e riforma: una sfida ecclesiale*, ed. R. Luciani, S. Noceti, and C. Schickendantz (Brescia: Queriniana, 2022), 250–70.

7. See S. Noceti, "Nuove coreografie. La pluralità ministerial necessaria per una liturgia viva e vitale," in *Ecclesia Orans* 39, no. 2 (2022): 496–503.

8. See my contribution "Reforma de la Iglesia, reforma del ministerio ordenado," in *Reforma de estructuras y conversion de mentalidades. Retos y desafios para una iglesia sinodal*, ed. R. Luciani and C. Schickendantz (Madrid: Ediciones Khaf, 2020), 313–46.

9. See E. Castellucci, "A trent'anni dal decreto 'Presbyterorum Ordinis.' La discussione teologica postconciliare sul ministero presbiterale," *La Scuola Cattolica* 124 (1996): 3–68; 195–261; K. Depoortere, "Ministry since Vatican II: From Sacerdos to Presbyter... And Back?," in *Vatican II and Its Legacy*, ed. L. Kenis and Lamberigts (Leuven: Peeters, 2002), 411–42; various authors, *Ministero presbiterale in trasformazione* (Brescia: Morcelliana, 2005); R. LaDelfa, "Il ministero presbiterale nei documenti del magistero dopo il Vaticano II," in *Il presbitero nella chiesa dopo il Vaticano II*, ed. P. Sorci (Trapani: Il Pozzo di Giacobbe, 2005), 127–44.

10. Congregatio pro clericis et al., "Ecclesiae de mysterio, Su alcune questioni circa la collaborazione dei laici al ministero dei sacerdoti," in *Enchiridion Vaticanum* 16/671–740; B. Sesboüé, *Rome et les laics. Une nouvelle pièce au débat: l'Instruction romaine du 15 août 1997* (Paris: Desclée de Brouwer, 1996); S. Noceti, "*Nuovi cammini per la ministerialità ecclesiale. Ermeneutiche magisteriali post-conciliari*," Path, *Pontifical Academy of Theology* 20, no. 1 (2021): 55–77.

11. Francis, apostolic letters, with issued motu proprio *Spiritus Domini* (January 10, 2021); and *Antiquum ministerium*, May 10, 2021, www.vatican.va.

12. See Brazilian Bishops' Conference, *Missão e ministerios dos cristãos leigos e leigas* (São Paulo: Paulinas, 1999); German Bishops' Conference, "Il servizio pastorale nelle parrocchie," *Il Regno documenti* 41 (1996): 160–67; United States Conference of Catholic Bishops, *Co-Workers in the Vineyard of the Lord. A Resource for Guiding the Develop-*

Notes

ment of Lay Ecclesial Ministry (Washington, DC: USCCB, 2005). See Z. Fox, ed., *Lay Ecclesial Ministry. Pathways Toward the Future* (Lanham, MD: Rowman & Littlefield, 2010); A.J. De Almeida, *Nuevos ministerios: Vocacion, carisma y servicio en la comunidad* (Barcelona: Herder, 2015).

13. On the theology of the laity at Vatican II, see G. Caracciolo, *Spiritualità e laicato nel Vaticano II e nella teologia del tempo* (Milan: Glossa, 2008); M. Vergottini, "I laici nel Vaticano II. Ermeneutica dei testi e recezione conciliare," in *La chiesa e il Vaticano II. Problemi di ermeneutica e recezione conciliare,* ed. M. Vergottini (Milan: Glossa, 2005), 331–58; G. Zambon, *Laicato e tipologie ecclesiali. Ricerca storica sulla "Teologia del laicato" in Italia alla luce del Vaticano II (1950–1980)* (Rome: PUG, 1991); M. Vergottini, *Il cristiano testimone. Congedo dalla teologia del laicato,* 3rd ed. (Bologna: EDB, 2018); M.T. Fernández Conde, *La misión profética de los laicos del Concilio Vaticano II a nuestros días. El laico "signo profético" en los ámbitos de la Iglesia y del mundo* (Rome: PUG, 2001); C. Masson, *Les laïcs dans le souffle du Concile* (Paris: Editions du Cerf, 2007); E. Palladino, *Laici e società contemporanea. Metodo e bilancio a cinquant'anni dal Vaticano II* (Assisi: Cittadella, 2013).

14. Francis, *Evangelii gaudium* 102.

15. *Lumen Gentium* 33; *Apostolicam Actuositatem* 20, 22, 24.

16. International Theological Commission (ITC), "Synodality in the Life and Mission of the Church," March 2, 2018; cited here is § 7, www.vatican.va; see also S. Madrigal, ed., *La sinodalidad en la vida y en la misión de la Iglesia* (Madrid: BAC, 2019).

17. See my contribution "Laity and Synodality: A Necessary Word," in *La Sinodalità*, 93–105.

18. ITC, "Synodality," 74.

19. ITC, "Synodality," 55.

20. ITC, "Synodality," 73.

21. On laity and synodality, see in particular, J.R. Villar, "Sinodalidad: Pastores y fieles en communion operativa," *Scripta Theologica* 48 (2016): 667–85; A. De Almeida, "Laicos y laicas en la práctica de la

sinodalidad," in *La sinodalidad en la vida de la Iglesia*, ed. R. Luciani and M.P. Silveira (Madrid: San Pablo, 2020), 243–76; L. Clavell, "The First Level of Synodality and Listening to the Voice of the Lay Faithful," in *A cinquant'anni dall'*Apostolica sollicitudo: *il *Sinodo dei Vescovi al servizio di una Chiesa sinodale. Acts of the study seminar organized by the General Secretariat of the Synod of Bishops (Vatican City, 6–9 February 2016)*, ed. L. Baldisseri (Vatican City: LEV, 2016), 299–306.

22. *Ad gentes* 21.

23. We must go beyond that vision, typical of the theology of the laity of the 1950s, present in some aspects also in the decree *Apostolicam Actuositatem* and in the fourth chapter of *Lumen Gentium*, which identifies the secular nature as the peculiar and exclusive characteristic of the laity. See S. Noceti, *Laici e* sensus fidei *(LG 12)*, in *I laici dopo il Concilio: quale autonomia*, ed. C. Militello (Bologna: EDB, 2012), 87–101.

24. ITC, "Synodality," 68: listening to the *voices of* the faithful.

25. See C. Pena García, "Ministerialidad laical en una Iglesia sinodal," in *En camino hacia una iglesia sinodal. De Pablo VI a Francisco*, ed. R. Luciani and M.T. Compte (Madrid: PPC, 2020), 305–46.

26. B. Hinze, "Can We Find a Way Together? The Challenge of Synodality in a Wounded and Wounding Church," *Irish Theological Quarterly* 85 (2020): 215.

27. We will elaborate on this in chapter 6.

28. See "Ministeri laicali," *Credere Oggi* 175 (2010): 1; Gruppo italiano docenti di diritto canonico, *I laici nella ministerialità della Chiesa* (Milan: Glossa, 1996); P. Neuner, *Per una teologia del popolo di Dio* (Brescia: Queriniana, 2016); A. Borras and G. Routhier, *Les nouveaux ministères: Diversité et articulation* (Montreal: Mediaspaul, 2009); D.M. Eschenauer and H.D. Horell, eds., *Reflections on Renewal: Lay Ecclesial Ministry and the Church* (Collegeville, MN: Liturgical Press, 2011); A. Parra, *I ministeri nella chiesa dei poveri* (Assisi: Cittadella, 1994); A.J. De Almeida, *Nuevos ministerios: Vocacion, carisma y servicio en la comunidad* (Barcelona: Herder, 2015).

Notes

29. See M. Vergottini, "Laici a tempo pieno nella pastorale," *Rivista del Clero Italiano*, 76 (1995): 288–99; A. Loretan, *Laien im pastoralen Dienst. Ein Amt in der kirchlichen Gesetzgebung: Pastoralassistent/- assistentin, Pastoralreferent/-referentin*, 2nd ed. (Freiburg: Universitätsverlag, 1994, 1997), 19–134; A. Montan, "Laical Assignments, Offices and Ministries in the Ecclesial Community," in *Servire ecclesiae*, ed. N. Ciola (Bologna: EDB, 1998), 555–78.

30. See A. Borras, ed., *Des laïcs en responsabilité pastorale? Accueillir de nouveaux ministères* (Paris: Editions du Cerf, 1998); and *Quando manca il prete. Aspetti teologici, canonici e pastorali* (Bologna: EDB, 2018); F. Moog, *La participation des laïcs à la charge pastorale* (Paris: Desclée de Brouwer, 2010).

31. See Paul VI, Apostolic Letter *Ministeria quaedam*, August 15, 1972, www.vatican.va; G. Max, "'*Ministeria quaedam*': A rereading in the light of the problematic and subsequent documents," *Rivista Liturgica* 94 (2007): 547–58; M. Kunzler, *Charisma e liturgia. Teologia e forma dei ministeri liturgici laicali* (Lugano: EU-Press, 2006); L. Sabbarese, *Ordini minori e ministeri nella legislazione della Chiesa, Ius Missionale* 7, no. 1 (2013): 225–57; E. Zanetti, "I ministeri laicali nel post-concilio: cifra di una chance e di un agio?," *Periodica de re canonica* 90 (2001): 591–611.

32. S. Noceti, "*Spiritus Domini* e *Antiquum ministerium*: un contributo alla riforma della Chiesa," *Il Regno attualità* 66 (2021) XII: 351–53; Noceti, *Per una chiesa dai molti ministeri*, *Il Regno attualità* 66 (2021) II: 8–10; A. Join-Lambert and A. Haquin, "Lectorat et acolytat pour les femmes. Transformer une évidence en opportunité pour le renouveau de l'Église," *Nouvelle Revue Theologique* 143 (2021): 256–65 (tr. en. Reader and acolyte open to women. Trasformare una evidenza in un'opportunità per la rinnovamento della chiesa, in *Rivista del clero italiano* [2021]: 396–405).

33. I have reflected on this theme in "Il munus regale dei laici (LG 36). Una prospettiva per comprendere la soggettualità dei laici secondo il concilio Vaticano II," in *Concilio e partecipazione laicale*, ed. A. Clemenzia (Florence: Nerbini, 2020), 35–48.

34. *Relatio* in AS III, no. 1, 291–292; cited by R. Tononi, "La funzione regale di Cristo e dei cristiani nella *Lumen gentium*," in *La funzione regale di Cristo e dei cristiani* (Brescia: Morcelliana, 1997), 207–37: 217.

35. See Code of Canon Law canons 129 and 228 for the foundation of subjectivity; see also ITC, "Synodality," 80, 102. See C. Pena Garcia, *Ministerialidad laical en una Iglesia sinodal*, 305–46.

36. On the theme of ministeriality at the Amazon Synod, see my contribution published in "Una chiesa tutta ministeriale. El Sínodo para la Amazonía y reflexión so los ministerios que 'fanno chiesa,'" *Urbaniana University Journal* 73, no. II (2020): 117–48; tr.sp. "El Sínodo para la Amazonía y la reflexión sobre los ministerios que 'hacen Iglesia,'" in *La sinodalidad en la vida de la Iglesia*, ed. R. Luciani and M. del Pilar Silveira (Madrid: San Pablo, 2020), 343–73.

37. Y. M. Congar, Intervention, in *Tous responsables dans l'église? Le ministère presbytéral dans l'église tout entière "ministérielle". Réflexions de l'assembléeplénière de l'Episcopat and Lourdes 1973* (Paris: Centurion, 1973), 60–61. See also M. Congar, *Ministries and Ecclesial Communion* (Bologna: EDB, 1976).

38. See "Ministries in the Church Today," *Concilium* 46, no. 1 (2010).

39. Amazon Synod, Final Document 79, 82. On the topic of ministries in the Amazon Synod, see my "Una chiesa tutta ministeriale."

40. Francis, *Querida Amazonia*, no. 94.

41. F. Lobinger, *Equipos de ministros ordenados*, ebook, kindle ed., pos. 123.

42. S. Segoloni, "Chiesa e questione femminile. Un caso serio per la sinodalità," in *Sinodalità*, ed. Battocchio and Tonello, 81–98; S. Martinez Cano, "Hablar de sinodalidad es cabla de mujeres," in *En camino hacia una iglesia* sinodal, eds Luciani and Compte, 347–68.

43. Francis, *Evangelii Gaudium* 103–4; *Christus Vivit* 42. See also *Amoris Laetitia* 54, 154. See also my "For an Inclusive Church (EG 103–4). Principles of an Ecclesiological Re/vision," in *Misericordia e tenerezza. The theological programme of Pope Francis*, ed. K. Appel and J.H. Deibl (Milan: San Paolo, 2019), 363–76.

Notes

44. See C.E. McEnroy, *Guests in Their Own House: The Women of Vatican II* (New York: Crossroad, 1996 [rev. ed. 2011]); M. Perroni, A. Melloni, and S. Noceti, eds., *Tantum aurora est. Donne e Concilio Vaticano II* (Munich: LIT Verlag, 2012); M. Eckholt, *Ohne die Frauen ist keine Kirche zu machen. Der Aufbruch des Konzils und die Zeichen der Zeit* (Mainz: Matthias Grünewald Verlag, 2012).

45. See A. Valerio, *Donne e Chiesa. Una storia di genere* (Rome: Carocci, 2016); Valerio, *Il potere delle donne nella Chiesa* (Bari: Laterza, 2016); L. Scaraffia and G. Zarri, eds., *Donne e fede* (Bari: Laterza, 1994).

46. This is the title of the first book by E. Schüssler Fiorenza, published in 1964, later taken up in the article, "The Forgotten Partner: The Professional Ministry of Women in the Church," in *Discipleship of Equals: A Critical Feminist Ekklesia-logy of Liberation* (New York: Herder & Herder, 1993), 13–22.

47. See C. Militello, ed., *Il Vaticano II e la sua recezione al femminile* (Bologna: EDB, 2007); M. Perroni and H. Legrand, eds., *Avendo qualcosa da dire. Teologhe e teologi rileggono il Vaticano II* (Milan: Paoline, 2014).

48. See K.E. Børresen, ed., *In the Image of God. Models of Gender in the Jewish and Christian Tradition* (Rome: Carocci, 2001).

49. C. Militello, "Sponsorship, Virginity and Motherhood, Ecclesiological Coordinates of *Mulieris Dignitatem*," *Convivium Assisiense* 11 (2009): 51–60.

50. See U. King and T. Beattie, *Gender, Religion, and Diversity: Cross-cultural Perspectives* (London: Bloomsbury Press, 2005); S. Ross, "Christian Anthropology and Gender Essentialism," *Concilium* 42 (2006): 60–68; M. Perroni, "A proposito del principio mariano-petrino," in *La fede e la sua comunicazione*, ed. P. Ciardella and S. Maggiani (Bologna: EDB, 2006), 93–116.

51. T. Berger, ed., *Liturgie und Frauenfrage. Ein Beitrag zur Frauenfrage aus liturgiewissenschaftlicher Sicht* (Landsberg: St. Ottilien, 1990).

52. See G. Prüller-Jagenteufel, and Bong, and R. Perintfalvi, eds., *Toward Just Gender Relations. Rethinking the Role of Women in Church and Society* (Göttingen: Vienna University Press, 2019); P. Zagano,

Women and Catholicism: Gender, Communion and Authority (New York: Macmillan, 2011); E. Schüssler Fiorenza, *Empowering Memory and Movement. Thinking and Working across Borders* (Minneapolis: Fortress Press, 2014).

53. E. Schüssler Fiorenza, *Discipleship of Equals* (New York: Herder & Herder, 1993).

54. I have presented my position at greater length in "Le donne e la chiesa cattolica: cittadini non ospiti. Uno sguardo sull'attualità," in *Genere e religioni. Un dialogo interdisciplinare,* ed. F. Bartolacci and I. Crespi and N. Mattucci (Rome: Aracne, 2020), 19–38; "Reformas que queremos las mujeres en la Iglesia," in *Reforma y reformas en la Iglesia. Miradas críticas de las mujeres cristianas* (Madrid 11–12 Nov. 2017), Asociación de Téologas Españolas (ATE), ed. M. Vidal (Estella: Editorial Verbo Divino, 2018); see also C. Militello and S. Noceti, eds., *Le donne e la riforma della Chiesa* (Bologna: EDB, 2017).

55. See *Concilium* 35 (1999) III: *The Non-ordination of Women and the Politics of Power;* I. Jones, J. Wootton, and Ch. Thorpe, eds., *Women and Ordination in the Christian Churches* (London/New York: T&T Clark, 2008); S. Noceti, *Donne e ministero: una questione scomoda. Orientations and Interpretative Perspectives In Theological Reflection on Women,* in A. Calapaj Burlini, ed., *Liturgia e ministeri ecclesiali* (Rome: Edizioni Liturgiche, 2008), 67–99; M. Eckholt et al., ed., *Frauen in kirchlichen Ämtern* (Freiberg: Herder, 2018).

56. P. Hünermann, ed., *Diakonat. Ein Amt für Frauen in der Kirche and ein frauengerechts Amt* (Ostfildern, 1997); G. Macy, W. T. Ditewig, and P. Zagano, *Women Deacons. Past, Present, Future* (New York / Mahwah, NJ: Paulist Press, 2011); C. Simonelli and M. Scimmi, *Women Deacons? La posta in gioco* (Padua: Messaggero, 2016); S. Noceti, ed., *Deacon. Quale ministero per quale chiesa?* (Brescia: Queriniana, 2017); S. Martínez Cano and C. Soto Varela, eds., *Mujeres y diaconado. Sobre los ministerios en la Iglesia* (Estella: Editorial Verbo Divino, 2019).

57. See C. Simonelli and M. Ferrari, eds., *Una chiesa di donne e uomini* (Camaldoli: Editiones di Camaldoli, 2015); various authors, "Donne invisibili nella teologia e nella chiesa," *Concilium* 21 (1985): vi.

Notes

58. See the solicitous and prophetic contribution of H. Häring, "Concluding Reflection: Women's Power: Future of the Church," *Concilium* 35 (1999): 565–74.

59. The "Maria 2.0" movement in Germany teaches a way forward for everyone: to show how essential the contribution of women is in ordinary pastoral life by suspending, for a month, the catechetical, liturgical, and administrative services provided by women in parishes (and thus effectively blocking pastoral life as a whole).

60. M. Rosaldo, "The Uses and the Abuses of Anthropology," *Signs* 5 (1980): 389–417.

61. Francis, *Christus Vivit* 42.

62. On the ministeriality of the couple, see V. Mauro, ed., *Sacramento del matrimonio e teologia: Un percorso interdisciplinare* (Milan: Glossa, 2014); M. Aliotta, *Il matrimonio* (Brescia: Queriniana, 2002); various authors, *Il matrimonio. Quaderni del seminario di Brescia* (Brescia: Morcelliana, 1999); W. Kasper, *Teologia del matrimonio cristiano* (Brescia: Queriniana, 1979 [orig. 1977]); L. Ligier, *Il matrimonio. Questioni teologiche e pastorali* (Rome: Città Nuova, 1988); R. Tagliaferri, *Dedicare la vita: il matrimonio e la famiglia*, in *Corso di teologia sacramentaria*, II, ed. A. Grillo, M. Perroni, and P.R. Tragan (Brescia: Queriniana, 2000), 226–82.

63. See Th. Knieps-Port Le Roy and A. Brenninkmeijer-Werhahn, eds., *Authentic Voices–Discerning Hearts: New Resources for the Church on Marriage and Family* (Zürich: LIT Verlag, 2016).

64. See K. Rahner, "Il matrimonio come sacramento," in *Nuovi Saggi*, vol. 3 (Rome: Paoline, 1968), 575–602.

65. I have developed this reading in S. Dianich and S. Noceti, *Trattato sulla chiesa*, 2nd ed. (Brescia: Queriniana, 2005), 417–28.

66. The expression entered the Second Vatican Council through the intervention of Msgr. P. Fiordelli (AS I/IV, 309–11; II/I, 794–95; II/III, 21–24). See M. Fahey, "The Christian Family as a Domestic Church according to the Second Vatican Council," *Concilium* 31 (1995): 129–39; Th. Knieps-Port Le Roy, G. Mannion, and P. De Mey,

eds., *The Household of God and Local Households. Revisiting the Domestic Church* (Leuven: Peeters, 2013).

67. See S. Noceti, "Reforma de la Iglesia, reforma del ministerio ordenado," in *Reforma de estructuras y conversion de mentalidadesi*, ed. R. Luciani and C. Schickendantz (Madrid: Ed. Khaf, 2020), 313–46; Noceti, "Nuovi ministeri per una riforma viva," *Credereoggi* 39 (2019) IV, 63–81.

68. On the theology of episcopacy and the ministry of the bishop according to Vatican II, see H. Legrand and Chr. Theobald, eds., *Le ministère des évêques au Concile Vatican II et depuis* (Paris: Cerf, 2001); M. Faggioli, *Il vescovo e il concilio. Modello episcopale e aggiornamento al Vaticano II* (Bologna: Il Mulino, 2005); P. Goyret, ed., *I vescovi e il loro ministero* (Vatican City: Libreria Editrice Vaticana, 2000); various authors, "Il Vescovo fra storia e teologia. Saggi in onore del card. S. Piovanelli," *Vivens Homo* 11 (2000) I; S. Noceti, "Il Concilio Vaticano II sull'autorità dei vescovi. Punti fermi e questioni aperte," in *Autorità e forme di potere nella chiesa*, ed. M. Epis (Milan: Glossa, 2019), 155–90.

69. G. Routhier, "A Forgotten Vision? The Function of Bishops and Its Exercise 40 years after the Second Vatican Council," *The Jurist* 69 (2009): 155–69.

70. Francis, *Episcopalis Communio* 5.

71. On the *tria munera*, see L. Schick, *Das dreifache Amt Christi und der Kirche: zur Entstehung und Entwicklung der Trilogien* (Frankfurt a.M: P. Lang, 1982); P. De Mey, "The Bishop's Participation in the Threefold *munera*," *The Jurist* 69 (2009): 31–58.

72. ITC, "Synodality," 69.

73. See S. Dianich, *La chiesa cattolica verso la sua riforma* (Brescia: Queriniana, 2014).

74. J. Gaudemet, *Les elections dans l'Eglise Latine des origines au XVI.e siécle* (Paris, 1979; J.I. González Faus, *"Ningún obispo impuesto." Las elecciones episcopales en la historia de la Iglesia* (Santander: Sal Terrae, 1992); M. Tkhorovskyy, *Procedura per la nominazione dei vescovi: evoluzione dal Codice del 1917 al Codice del 1983* (Rome: PUG, 2004).

Notes

75. M. Faggioli and S. Noceti, "*Christus Dominus*. Introduction and Commentary," in *Commentary on the Documents of Vatican II*, ed. S. Noceti and R. Repole, vol. 4 (Bologna: EDB, 2017), at 107–110.

76. In *PL* 50, 434 and *PL* 54, 634, respectively.

77. N. Timms and K. Wilson, eds., *Governance and Authority in the Roman Catholic Church* (London: SPCK, 2000).

78. See M. Bafuidinsoni, *Le Munus Regendi de l'evêque diocesain comme "munus Patris et pastoris" selon le concile Vatican II*, diss. Gregoriana, Rome 1999; C. La Piana and M. Crociata, "Il munus regendi del vescovo. Personal Mediation and the Structure of Diocesan Pastoral Care," in "*Ubi Petrus. Ibi ecclesia.*" *Sui sentieri del Concilio Vaticano II*, ed. M. Sodi (Rome: LAS, 2007), 447–69; P. Goyret, *El obispo, pastor de la Iglesia. Estudio teológico del munus regendi en* Lumen Gentium 27 (Pamplona: Ediciones Universidad de Navarra,1998); S. Noceti, "Il ministero del vescovo nel cambiamento," *Il Regno* 13 (2020): 434–43.

79. Cyprian, Ep. 14, also quoted by ITC, "Synodality," 22.

80. H.M. Legrand, "I ministeri nella chiesa locale," in *Iniziazione alla pratica della teologia*, vol. 3 (Brescia: Queriniana, 1986), 186–283, 339–52; S. Dianich, *Teologia del ministero ordinato. Un'interpretazione ecclesiologica*, 2nd ed. (Rome: Paoline, 1984); E. Castellucci, "A trent'anni dal decreto 'Presbyterorum Ordinis': La discussione teologica postconciliare sul ministero presbiterale," *La Scuola Cattolica* 124 (1996): 3–68, 195–261; various authors, *Ministero presbiterale in trasformazione* (Brescia: Morcelliana, 2005).

81. A. Borras, *Il diaconato vittima della sua novità?* (Bologna: EDB, 2008).

82. L. Garbinetto, *Preti e diaconi insieme. Per una nuova immagine di ministri nella Chiesa* (Bologna: EDB, 2018); L. Garbinetto and S. Noceti, eds., *Diaconato e diaconia. Per essere corresponsabili nella Chiesa* (Bologna: EDB, 2018); L. Bertelli, *Diaconato presbiterato episcopato. Un unico sacramento in prospettiva trinitaria* (Vicenza: ISG, 2019); S. Sander, *Gott begegnet im Anderen: der Diakon und die Einheit des sakramentalen Amtes* (Freiburg: Herder, 2006).

83. On the presidency of the celebration, see P. Sorci, "Il ministero presbiterale: presidenza dell'eucaristia e presidenza della comunità," in *Il presbitero nella chiesa dopo il Vaticano II*, ed. P. Sorci (Trapani: Il Pozzo di Giacobbe, 2005), 343–75; P. Caspani, "Ministero ordinato e presidenza dell'eucaristia," in *Presbiteri nel popolo di Dio. A servizio della comunione*, ed. M. Paleari and F. Scanziani (Milan: Àncora, 2015), 15–40; L. Girardi, "Il sacramento dell'ordine e la fisionomia del presbitero," *Esperienza e Teologia* 24 (2008): 9–30; L.-M. Chauvet, "La presidenza liturgica oggi: dal mistero al ministero," in *Assemblea santa. Forms, Presences, Presidency*, ed. G. Boselli (Bose: Qiqajon, 2009), 257–78; J. Baldovin, "The Eucharist and Ministerial Leadership," *CTSA Proceedings* 52 (1997): 63–81.

84. See F. Mandreoli, "Note di riflessione contextuale sulla teologia del diaconato," *Rivista di Teologia dell'Evangelizzazione* 12 (2008): 9–41; A. Haquin and Ph. Weber, eds., *Diaconat, XXIe siècle. Actes du Colloque de Louvain-la-Neuve (13–15 septembre 1994)* (Brussels: Lumen Vitae, 1997); R. Hartmann, , F. Reger, and S. Sander, eds., *Ortsbestimmungen: Der Diakonat als kirchlicher Dienst*, 2nd ed. (Freiburg: Herder, 2015); J.M. Barnett, *The Diaconate. A Full and Equal Order* (Harrisburg, PA: Trinity Press International, 1995); D. Vitali, *Diaconi, che fare?* (Milan: San Paolo, 2019); H. Legrand, "Le diaconat: renouveau et théologie," *Revue de Sciences philosophiques et theologiques* 69 (1985): 101–24.

85. I put forward my own line of interpretation of the diaconate in S. Noceti, "Il ministero dei diaconi tra teologia ed esperienze pastorali," in *Uomini che servono. Deacons of the diocese of Padua,* ed. A. Castegnaro and M. Chilese (Padua: Messaggero, 2015), 229–56.

86. See R.K. Greenleaf, *Servant Leadership. A Journey into the Nature of Legitimate Power and Greatness* (New York / Mahwah, NJ: Paulist Press, 1991). See also W.T. Ditewig, "The Kenotic Leadership of Deacons," in *The Deacon Reader*, ed. J. Keating (New York / Mahwah, NJ: Paulist Press, 2006), 248–77; Ditewig, *The Emerging Diaconate: Servant Leaders in a Servant Church* (New York / Mahwah, NJ: Paulist Press, 2007).

Notes

87. For seminary reform, see E. Brancozzi, *Rifare i preti, come ripensare i seminari* (Bologna: EDB, 2021); M. Guasco, "La formazione del clero: i seminari," in *Storia d'Italia, Annali, IX: La Chiesa e il potere politico dal Medioevo all'età contemporanea* (Turin: Einaudi, 1986), 629–715; and *Seminari e clero nel '900* (Turin: Paoline, 1990); *La formazione del clero* (Milan: Jaca Book, 2002).

88. As LG 27 states: "*Episcopi Ecclesias particulares sibi commissas ut vicarii et legati Christi regunt, consiliis, suasionibus, exemplis, verum etiam auctoritate et sacra potestate, qua quidem nonnisi ad gregem suum in veritate et sanctitate aedificandum utuntur, memores quod qui maior est fiat sicut minor et qui praecessor est sicut ministrator (cf. Lc 22,26–27)*."

89. See R. Repole, "Il vescovo nel suo presbiterio. Ripensare oggi la realtà del presbiterio," *Rivista del clero italiano* 98 (2017): 405–19; G. Frausini, *Il presbiterio. It Is Not Good for the Bishop to be Alone* (Assisi: Cittadella, 2007); P. Preaux, *Les fondements ecclésiologiques du presbyterium* (Frankfurt-Berlin-Bern: Lang, 2002).

90. See L. Tonello, *Il "gruppo ministeriale" parrocchiale* (Padua: EMP-FTTR, 2008); L. Fontolan and L. Tonello, *Agire in équipe nei gruppi ministeriali* (Trapani: Il Pozzo di Giacobbe, 2014).

91. See S. Noceti, "On the Pontificate of Pope Francis. The Keys to Reform: Starting with Leadership," *Il Regno attualità* 64 (2019) VIII, 249–52.

92. F. Lobinger, *Equipos de ministros ordenados,* ebook, kindle ed., pos. 123.

CHAPTER 4

1. International Theological Commission (ITC), "Synodality in the Life and Mission of the Church," no. 67.

2. ITC, "Synodality," 22.

3. On co-responsibility, in addition to the text already cited by L. Tonello, see O. Bobineau and J. Guyon, eds., *Corresponsabilité dans l'église, utopie o realisme?* (Paris: Desclée de Brouwer, 2010) and

my two contributions "New Ministries for a Living Reform," *Credere Oggi* 232, no. 4 (2019): 63–81; "Sfidati alla corresponsabilità: laici e ministri ordinati, insieme nel servizio ecclesiale," *Credere Oggi* 175, no. 1 (2010): 47–61.

4. See L. de Kerimel, *En finir avec le cléricalisme* (Paris: Seuil, 2020); G. Wilson, *Clericalism: The Death of the Priesthood* (Collegeville, MN: Liturgical Press, 2008).

5. See D. Menozzi, "Clericalism. Storia di una parola," *Il Regno* 65 (2020): 233–35.

6. See A. Lebra, "Clericalismo," *Settimana News*, September 24, 2020, http://www.settimananews.it/chiesa/clericalismo-2/.

7. See C. Schickendantz, "Elitismo y clericalismo. La conversión sinodal y la crisis de los abusos," in *Reforma de estructuras y conversion de mentalidades. Retos y desafios para una iglesia sinodal*, ed. R. Luciani and C. Schickendantz (Madrid: Khaf, 2020), 231–58.

8. See "Pact of the Catacombs" signed on November 16, 1965, by forty Council Fathers; see X. Pikaza and J. Antunes da Silva, eds., *El Pacto de las Catacumbas. La misión de los pobres en la Iglesia* (Estella: Editorial Verbo Divino, 2015).

9. See J. Friedmann, *Empowerment. Verso il potere di tutti* (Torre dei Nolfi, Italy: Edizioni Qualevita, 2004); N. Wolf, *Fire with Fire. The New Female Power and How to Use It* (New York: Fawcett Books, 1994); F. Vaccarini, *Pedagogia, potere ed empowerment* (Pedagogy, Power and Empowerment) (ebook, July 4, 2014); B. Vallerie, ed., *Interventions sociales et empowerment* (Paris: L'Harmattan, 2012); M.H. Bacqué and C. Biewener, *L'empowerment, une pratique émancipatrice?* (Paris: La Decouverte, 2015).

10. See H. Legrand, "Synodality, an Inherent Dimension of Ecclesial Life. Foundations and Actuality," *Vivens Homo* 16 (2005): 7–42; ITC, "Synodality," 64, 106.

11. See B. Major, "Gender Difference in Comparisons and Entitlement," *Journal of Social Issues* 45, no. 4 (1989): 99–115; E. Singer, "Reference Groups and Social Evaluations," in *Social Psychology*, ed. M. Rosenberg (New York: Transaction, 1981), 66–93.

Notes

12. See G. Richi Alberti, "Sinodalidad y carisma en la Iglesia," in *En camino hacia una iglesia sinodal*, ed. R. Luciani and M.T. Compte, 327–46; M. Nardello, *I carismi forma dell'esistenza cristiana. Identity and Discernment* (Bologna: EDB, 2012).

13. Italian Bishops' Conference, "Comunicare il Vangelo in un mondo che cambia" (Communicating the Gospel in a Changing World), June 29, 2001, 54.

14. E. Sampson, "Foundations for a Textual Analysis of Selfhood," in *Texts of Identity*, ed. J. Shotter and K. Gegen (London: Sage, 1989), 14 (cited by S. Gherardi, *Il genere e le organizzazioni*, 123).

15. The literature on the subject of power is vast. For a general introduction to the issues debated and the exercise of authority and power in the life of the church, see B. Barnes, *La natura del potere* (Bologna: Il Mulino, 1995 [orig. 1988]); R. d'Ambrosio, *Il potere e chi lo detiene* (Bologna: EDB, 2008); G. Mannion, "What Do We Mean by 'Authority'?," in *Authority in the Roman Catholic Church. Theory and Practice*, ed. B. Hoose (Aldershot: Ashgate, 2002), 19–36; G. Mannion, R. Gaillardetz, an J. Kerkohs, and K. Wilson, *Readings in Church Authority* (Aldershot: Ashgate, 2003); M.N. Ebertz, "Dienstamt, Macht, Herrschaft in Kirche und Gesellschaft," in *Amt und Autorität*, ed. M. Remenyi (Paderborn: Schöningen, 2012), 115–38; K.A. Pasewark, *A Theology of Power: Being Beyond Domination* (Minneapolis: Fortress, 1993).

16. ITC, "Synodality," 67.

17. V. Twyford, S. Waters, M. Hardy, and J. Dengate, *The Power of 'Co': The Smart Leaders' Guide to Collaborative Governance* (Woolongong, Australia: Vivien Twyford Communication Pty. Ltd., 2012), ebook.

18. See S. Noceti, "Co-responsible in the Church. Una riflessione a partire da Ef 4,11–16," in *Diaconato e diaconia. Per essere corresponsabili nella chiesa*, ed. L. Garbinetto and S. Noceti (Bologna: EDB, 2018), 107–15.

19. Ch. Perrot, *Ministers and Ministries. Investigation in the Christian Communities of the New Testament* (Milan: San Paolo, 2002), 5.

20. See A. Bryman, D. Collison, K. Grint et al., eds., *The Sage Handbook of Leadership* (London: Sage, 2011); D. Campus, *The Leader's Style. Deciding and Communicating in Contemporary Democracies* (Bologna: Il Mulino, 2016); G.A. Yukl, *Leadership in Organizations* (Englewood Cliffs, NJ: Prentice-Hall, 1981); L. Angelini et al., *Nuovi modelli di leadership partecipativa* (Milan: Guerini, 2021); V. De Giosa, *Leadership. Theory and Practice of Organisation* (Rome: Carocci, 2010).

21. See J.M. Burns, *Transforming Leadership* (New York: Grove, 2003); N.M. Tichy and M.A. Devanna, *The Transformational Leader* (New York/Toronto: J. Wiley, 1990).

22. J.S. Nye, Jr., *Leadership and Power* (Bari: Laterza, 2010).

23. See S. Noceti, "On the Pontificate of Pope Francis. The Keys to Reform: Starting with Leadership," *Il Regno Attualità* 64, no. 8 (2019): 249–52.

24. B. Sesboüé, *N'ayez pas peur! Regards sur l'Église et les ministéres aujourd'hui* (Paris: Desclée de Brouwer, 1996), 174–75.

25. The two quotations are taken from D. Bonhoeffer, *Etica* (Brescia: Queriniana, 1995), 188–189; *Resistenza e resa* (Milan: Paoline, 1988), 64.

CHAPTER 5

1. S. Xeres, *La chiesa, Corpo inquieto. Duemila anni di storia sotto il segno della riforma* (Milan: Ancora, 2003).

2. On the reforms that took place in the church one can read C. Bellitto and D.Z. Flanagin, *Reassessing Reform: A Historical Investigation into Church Renewal* (Washington, DC: Catholic University of America Press, 2012); J. O'Malley, "Developments, Reforms, and Two Great Reformations," in *Tradition and Transition: Historical Perspectives on Vatican II* (Wilmington: DE: Glazier, 1989), 82–125; G.B. Ladner, *The Idea of Reform: Its Impact on Christian Thought and Action in the Age of the Fathers* (Cambridge, MA: Harvard University Press, 1959 [ed. Eugene, OR: Wipf and Stock, 2004]).

Notes

3. K. Rahner, *Trasformazione strutturale della chiesa come chance e come compito* (Brescia: Queriniana, 1973 [orig. 1972]); for the sociological perspective, see N. Brunsson, *Reform and Routine. Organizational Change and Stability in the Modern World* (Oxford: Oxford University Press, 2009); M. Ferrante and S. Zan, *Il fenomeno organizzativo*, 11th ed. (Rome: Carocci, 2007), 214–50; J.G. March and J.P. Olsen, *Rediscovering Institution. The Organizational Basis of Politics* (New York: Free Press, 1989); J.G. March, *Explorations in Organizations* (Stanford, CA: Stanford University Press, 2008), 191–296); G.R. Bushe and R.J. Marshak, eds., *Dialogic Organization Development* (Oakland, CA: Barrett and Köhler), 2015.

4. An essential point of reference remains Y.M. Congar, *Vera e falsa riforma nella chiesa* (Milan: Jaca Book, 1972 [orig. 1950]).

5. Brunsson, *Reform and Routine*, 6.

6. I have developed the theme of church reform in "Church Reform. Indispensable and, Now, Possible," *Il Regno-Attualità* 61 (2016): 681–90; "Women and Church Reform," in *Le donne e la riforma della chiesa*, ed. C. Militello and S. Noceti (Bologna: EDB, 2017), 27–43; "Reformas que queremos las mujeres en la Iglesia," in *Reforma y reformas en la Iglesia. Miradas críticas de las mujeres cristianas (Madrid, Nov. 11–12, 2017)*, ed. Asociación de Téologas Españolas (ATE) and M. Vidal (Estella: Editorial Verbo Divino, 2018).

7. See S. Noceti, "What Structures for a Church in Reform?," *Concilium* 54 (2018): 652–68; C. Schickendantz, *Cambios estructral de la Iglesia como tarea y oportunidad* (Cordoba: Ed. Universidad Catolica de Cordoba, 2005).

8. See J.A. Komonchak, "La realizzazione locale della chiesa," in *Il Vaticano II e la chiesa*, ed. G. Alberigo and J.P. Jossua (Brescia: Paideia, 1985), 107–25; H.M. Legrand, "La realizzazione della chiesa in un luogo," in *Initiation to the Practice of Theology*, ed. B. Lauret and F. Refoulé, vol. 3 (Brescia: Queriniana, 1986), 147–335, in particular 155–76; J.M.R. Tillard, *L'église locale* (Paris: Cerf, 1995), 284–91. In this volume, we will use the expression *local church* to indicate the diocese, unlike CD 11 and the 1983 Code of Canon Law, which use the adjective *particular*.

9. See M. Fallert, *Mitarbeiter der Bischöfe: Das zueinander des bischöflichen und priesterlichen Amtes auf und nach dem Zweiten Vatikanischen Konzil* (Würzburg: Echter, 2007); H. Legrand and Chr. Theobald, eds., *Le ministère des évêques au Concile Vatican II et depuis* (Paris: Cerf, 2001); M. Faggioli, *Il vescovo e il concilio. Modello episcopale e aggiornamento al Vaticano II* (Bologna: Il Mulino, 2005); S. Noceti, "Il Concilio Vaticano II sull'autorità dei vescovi," *Vivens Homo* 30 (2019): 113–40.

10. See S. Noceti, "Commentary on *Christus Dominus*," in *Commentary on the Documents of Vatican II, IV. Christus Dominus. Optatam Totius, Presbyterorum Ordinis*, ed. S. Noceti and R. Repole (Bologna: EDB, 2017), 41–189.

11. Numerous proposals for reform of the church and in the church have been formulated since the immediate postconciliar period; see among these for our theme: M. Kehl, *Dove va la chiesa? Una diagnosi del nostro tempo* (Brescia: Queriniana, 1998 [orig. 1996]); J. B. Libanio, *Scenari di chiesa* (Padua: Messaggero, 2002 [orig. 1999]); C. Duquoc, *Credo la chiesa. Precarious Institutions and the Kingdom of God* (Brescia: Queriniana, 2001); G. Lafont, *La chiesa. Il travaglio delle riforme* (Milan: San Paolo, 2012); S. Dianich, *La chiesa cattolica verso la sua riforma* (Brescia: Queriniana, 2014). On the synodal form of church focus, see many of the contributions of the seminar held at *La Civiltà Cattolica* in 2015, see A. Spadaro and C.M. Galli, eds., *La riforma e le riforme nella chiesa* (Brescia: Queriniana, 2016); S. Kopp, ed., *Kirche im Wandel. Ekklesiale Identität und Reform* (Freiburg: Herder, 2020).

12. Francis, "Address on the Occasion of the Commemoration of the 50th Anniversary of the Institution of the Synod of Bishops," October 17, 2015, www.vatican.va.

13. Consequently, in *Episcopalis communio*, art. 6 §1, it is stated that the consultation of the people of God takes place in the local churches.

14. ITC, "Synodality," 77–82 (first references to nos. 59, 61). See the commentary in canonical perspective by J. San José Prisco, "Las estructuras de la sinodalidad en la iglesia local," in *La sinodalidad en la*

Notes

vida y en la misión de la Iglesia, ed. S. Madrigal (Madrid: BAC, 2019), 141–74.

15. E. Lanne, "L'èglise locale et l'èglise universelle," in *Tradition et Communion des Eglises. Recueil D'etudes,* vol. 129, Bibliotheca Ephemeridum Theologicarum Lovaniensium (Leuven: Peeters, 1997), 490.

16. K. Rahner, "Il nuovo volto della chiesa," in *Nuovi saggi,* vol. 3 (Rome: EP, 1969 [orig. 1966]), 406.

17. See G. Routhier, "La Synodalité de l'Eglise Locale," *Studia Canonica* 26 (1992): 111–61; and "Il rinnovamento della vita sinodale nelle chiese locali," in *La riforma e le riforme nella chiesa,* ed. A. Spadaro and C.M. Galli (Brescia: Queriniana, 2016), 233–47.

18. See "Synodality: a Reflection from an Ecclesiological Perspective," in *La sinodalità al tempo di papa Francesco,* ed. N. Salato, vol. 1 (Bologna: EDB, 2020), 153–69; "Forma sinodale di chiesa," in *Forma e forme della chiesa. Per una chiesa estroversa,* ed. A. Clemenzia (Florence: Nerbini, 2020), 61–72; R. Luciani, "Sinodo e sinodalità. Tempo di conversione, tempo di riforma," *Il Regno Attualità* 2 (2022): 57–64.

19. See Code of Canon Law, c.396 §1; Directory, *Apostolorum Successores* 222–25.

20. See B. Zani, P. Selleri, and D. David, *La comunicazione. Modelli teorici e contesti sociali* (Rome: Carocci, 1998, 2007); G.K. Wilkins, Th. Tufte, and R. Obregon, eds., *The Handbook of Development Communication and Social Change* (Chichester, UK: Blackwell, 2014); S. Dianich, "Teorie della comunicazione ed ecclesiologia," in *L'ecclesiologia contemporanea,* ed. D. Valentini (Padua: Messaggero, 1994), 134–78; A. Toniolo, "Processi comunicativi e partecipativi nella Chiesa locale: prospettiva teologico-pastorale," in *Church and Synodality. Conscienza, forme,* processi, ed. R. Battocchio and S. Noceti (Milan: Glossa, 2007), 163–79; P. Granfield, ed., *The Church and Communication* (Kansas City: Sheed & Ward, 1994).

21. See D.K. Mumby, *Organizational Communication. A Critical Introduction,* 2nd ed. (London: Sage, 2013, 2018) ; G. Alessandrini, *Comunicare organizzando. La competenza comunicativa nell'organizzazione condivisa* (Rome: Seam, 1996).

22. See P. Berger and Th. Luckmann, *La realtà come costruzione sociale* (Bologna: Il Mulino, 1969), 132–47, 179–83.

23. See L.L. Putnam and D.K. Mumby, eds., *Handbook of Organizational Communication* (London: Sage, 2014), 103–5.

24. See F.R. Aznar, "La nueva concepción global de la curia diocesana en el Concilio Vaticano II," *Revista Española de Derecho Canónico* 36 (1980): 419–47; G. Marchetti, *La curia come organo di partecipazione alla cura pastorale del vescovo* (Rome: PUG, 2004).

25. A. Borras has given numerous indications for such a renewal; see in particular A. Borras, *Ecclesial Synodality, Participatory Processes and Decision-Making. Il punto di vista di un canonista,* in A. Spadaro and C.M. Galli, eds., *La riforma e le riforme nella chiesa* (Brescia: Queriniana, 2016), 207–32. See also S. Segoloni, "Chiesa e sinodalità: indagine sulla struttura ecclesiale a partire dal Vaticano II," *Convivium Assisiense* 14 (2012): 55–77; 15 (2013): 107–44: and U. Sartorio, *Sinodalità* (Milan: Ancora, 2020).

26. Italian Bishops' Conference, Pastoral Note *Con il dono della carità dentro la storia,* May 26, 1996, 21.

27. Synod of Bishops for the Pan-Amazonian Region, "Final Document—The Amazon: New Paths for the Church and for an Integral Ecology," October 26, 2019, 88, 90, www.vatican.va.

28. ITC, "Synodality," 78–79.

29. See G. Routhier, *Le Synode diocésain: le comprendre, le vivre, le célébrer* (Toronto: Novalis, 1995); H.M. Legrand, "Synodes et conseils de l'après-concile," *Nouvelle Revue Theologique* 98 (1976): 193–216; J.H. Provost, "The Ecclesiological Nature and Function of the Diocesan Synod in the Real Life of the Church," in *La synodalité. La participation au gouvernement dans l'Eglise,* vol. 2 (Paris: l'Année canonique, 1992), 537–58; A. Borras, "Trois expressions de la synodalité depuis Vatican II," *Ephemerides Theologicae Lovanienses* 90 (2014): 643–66; E. Cappellini and G.G. Sarzi Sartori, *The Diocesan Synod. History, Legislation, Experience* (Milan: San Paolo, 1994); A. Join-Lambert, *L'innovation inachevée du synode diocésain par et après le concile Vatican II,* in *Sinodalità e riforma. Una sfida ecclesiale,* ed. R. Luciani, S. Noceti,

and C. Schickendantz (Brescia: Queriniana, 2022); Join-Lambert, ed., *Synodes diocésains, "parasynodes" et conciles particuliers dans l'Église catholique depuis le Concile Vatican II, Liste, bibliographie, resources*, 6th ed. (Louvain/Paris/Quebec: Cahiers Internationaux de Teologie Pratique, 2016); H.M. Legrand, "Synodes et conseils de l'après-concile,", *Nouvelle Revue Théologique* 98 (1976): 193–216; J. Galea-Curmi, *The Diocesan Synod as a Pastoral Event. A Study of the Post-conciliar Understanding of the Diocesan Synod* (Rome: PUL, 2005).

30. See A. Join-Lambert, "Les processus synodaux depuis le concile Vatican II: une double expérience de l'Église et de l'Esprit Saint," *Cristianesimo nella storia* 32, no. 3 (2011): 1137–78.

31. *Ecclesiae Imago* 163; *Apostolorum Successores* 167.

32. See Congregation for Bishops/Congregation for the Evangelisation of Peoples, Instruction, *De Synodi Diocesanis Agendis*, 1997, www.vatican.va.

33. The first diocesan synod we know of is that of Auxerre, convened by Bishop Aunarius/Aunacharius (ca. 540–ca. 603).

34. See A. Longhitano, "La normativa sul Sinodo diocesano dal Concilio di Trento al Codice di Diritto Canonico," *La Scuola Cattolica* 115 (1987): 3–71.

35. First indication in *Ecclesiae Imago* 163, which supersedes the Code of 1917.

36. *Apostolorum Successores* 167 indicates that the aim is only to apply and adapt the universal discipline.

37. See E. Duffy, "Processes for Communal Discernment. Diocesan Synods and Assemblies," *The Jurist* 71 (2011): 77–90.

38. See M. Visioli, "Il sinodo diocesano: atto di governo episcopale ed evento di comunione. Aspetti canonistici," in *La Sinodalità*, ed. Battocchio and Tonello, 121–40; and "Una forma privilegata di produzione normativa nella chiesa locale: il sinodo diocesano," *Ephemerides Iuris Canonici* 57 (2017): 81–88.

39. See Borras, "Trois expressions de la synodalité," 655.

40. See Code of Canon Law, cc. 466, 460. See A. Montan, "Il vescovo pastore del suo popolo: la sinodalità diocesana (*Pastores gregis*,

42–54)," *Lateranum* 71 (2005): 545–61. The bishop is the only legislator for his diocese (canon 391); he is the only one who gives form of law to the decrees (c. 466); it is up to the bishop to guarantee to the laity and to the presbyterate freedom of thought, research, and speech, so that they may actively participate in the elaboration of the norms and documents, which the bishop will then promulgate.

41. See A. Longhitano, ed., "Repraesentatio: sinodalità ecclesiale e integrazione politica," in *Atti del Convegno di studio organizzato dallo Studio teologico di Catania e dalla Facoltà di Giurisprudenza dell'Università degli studi di Catania (quaderni di Synaxis)* (Florence: Giunti, 2007).

42. L. Bressan, "Sinodi diocesani: luoghi di sinodalità?," in *Chiesa e sinodalità: Coscienza forme processi,* eds. R. Battocchio and S. Noceti (Milan: Glossa, 2007), 273–92.

43. Congregation for Bishops/Congregation for the Evangelisation of Peoples, *De synodis diocesanis agendis* (1997) 2.

44. R. Repole, "Il Sinodo diocesano: una prospettiva teologica," in *La Synodalità*, ed. Battocchio and Tonello, 97–120.

45. Duffy, *Processes for Communal Discernment*, 90.

46. See E. Miragoli, *Il consiglio pastorale diocesano secondo il Concilio Vaticano II e la sua attuazione nelle diocesi lombarde* (Rome: PUG, 1996), 5–55; A. Borras, "Sinodalità ecclesiale, processi partecipativi e modalità decisionali. Il punto di vista di un canonista," in *La riforma e le riforme nella chiesa*, ed. A. Spadaro and C.M. Galli, 207–32; P. Gherri, *Discernere e scegliere nella chiesa* (Rome: Lateran University Press, 2016); S. Segoloni, "Consultare e consigliare nella chiesa. La stagione conciliare moderna," *Apollinaris* 87 (2015): 487–549; M. Rivella, ed., *Partecipazione e corresponsabilità nella chiesa. I consigli diocesani e parrocchiali* (Milan: Ancora, 2000); S. Berlingò, "I Consigli pastorali," in *La Synodalité. La participation au gouvernement dans l'église*, vol. 2 (Paris: UNESCO, 1997), 717–44. In the volume *La Synodalità*, ed. Battocchio and Tonello, see the contributions on *Il consiglio pastorale diocesano e parrocchiale*, in prospettiva ecclesiologica (V. Mignozzi, pp. 141–52), in

prospettiva pastorale (L. Tonello, pp. 153–70), in prospettiva canonistica (A. Giraudo, pp. 171–81).

47. Code of Canon Law, c. 511. *Apostolorum successores* 84 judges that "it is good that there should be."

48. Code of Canon Law, c. 514 §2, generically states "at least once a year."

49. B. David, "Les Conseils paroissiaux," *Les Cahiers du droit ecclesial* 3, no. 8 (1986): 12. In the Code of Canon Law, c. 512: "the portion of the people of God who look after the diocese, bearing in mind the different areas of the diocese, the social conditions, the professions, and also the role they play in the apostolate, either as individuals or as associates."

50. See A. Borras, "Votum tantum consultivum. Les limites ecclésiologiques d'une formule canonique," *Didaskalia* 45 (2015): 145–62; F. Coccopalmerio, "La 'consultivit à' del consiglio pastorale parrocchiale e del Consiglio per gli affari economici della parrocchia," *Quaderni di Diritto Ecclesiale* 1 (1988): 60–65.

51. See Mignozzi, *The Diocesan and Parish Pastoral Council. Notes of an Ecclesiological Nature*, 150–51.

52. ITC, "Synodality," 81.

53. J.J. Arrieta, "El régimen jurídico de los Consejos presbiteral y pastoral," *Jus Canonicum* 21 (1981): 567–605; L. Martinez Sistach, "Consejo presbiteral y asambleas diocesanas de presbíteros," in *La Curia Episcopal. Reforma y actualización* (Salamanca: Univ. Salamanca, 1979), 133–72; G. Incitti, *Il consiglio presbiterale. Alle origini di una crisi* (Bologna: Dehoniane, 1996); T. Pieronek, "Natura e funzione del Consiglio presbiterale," in *La Synodalité. La partecipation au gouvernement dans l'Eglise, Actes du VIIme Congrés International de Droit Canonique, Paris 21–28 September 1990*, in *L'Année Canonique* (1992) I–II, hors série.

54. The Presbyteral Council is mandatory.

55. Canon 500 §2 provides that the vote of the presbyteral council has a consultative value, and that the bishop needs the consent of this council only in the cases provided for by law.

56. E. Castellucci, "Commentary on *Presbyterorum ordinis* 7," in *Commentary on the Documents of the Second Vatican Council*, ed. S. Noceti and R. Repole, vol. 4 (Bologna: EDB, 2017), 402–8, at 406.

57. ITC, "Synodality," 80, 81.

58. A. Borras, "Synodalité ecclésiale, processus partecipatif et modalités decisionnelles," in *Communion ecclesiale et synodalité* (Paris: CLD Editions, 2018), 157–74 at 166; see also "L'eveque diocesain, son Conseil Episcopal et le Conseil Presbyteral au service du governement du diocese," *Studia Canonica* 139 (2015): 111–38.

59. See L. Bressan, *La parrocchia oggi. Identity, Transformations, Challenges* (Bologna: EDB, 2004); various authors, *La parrocchia. Tra desiderio di identità e urgenza di cambiamento* (Milan: Glossa, 2006); L. Bressan and L. Diotallevi, *Tra le case degli uomini, presente e "possibilità" della parrocchia italiana* (Assisi: Cittadella Editrice, 2006); *La parrocchia come chiesa locale* (Morcelliana, Brescia: Quaderni teologici del Seminario di Brescia, 1993).

60. See P.V. Aimone, "La parrocchia nel secondo millennio," in Gruppo Italiano Docenti di Diritto Canonico, *La parrocchia* (Milan: Glossa, 2005), 35–86; P. Cozzo, *Andate in pace. Parroci e parrocchie in Italia dal Concilio di Trento a papa Francesco* (Rome: Carocci Editore, 2014).

61. See G. Zanchi, *Rimessi in viaggio. Immagini da una chiesa che verrà* (Milan: Vita e Pensiero, 2019); "La chiesa che verrà," *Credere Oggi* 232, no. 4 (2019); "La chiesa del futuro," *Concilium* 54, no. 4 (2018). For a new inculturation of church in the European context, see my "Reformation and Inculturation of the Church in Europe," in *La riforma e le riforme nella chiesa*, ed. A. Spadaro and C.M. Galli, 504–20.

62. See V. Bo, *Storia della parrocchia*, vols. 1–5, (Rome: Dehoniane, 1988–1994 [new editions EDB, Bologna]); S. Dianich, "L'ecclesiologia della parrocchia," *Il Regno Attualità* 12 (2003): 418–25.

63. R. Luciani, S. Noceti, and C. Schickendantz, eds., *Synodalità e riforma: una sfida ecclesiale* (Brescia: Queriniana, 2022); A. Toniolo, "Processi comunicativi e partecipativi nella Chiesa locale: prospettiva teologico-pastorale," in *Chiesa e sinodalità. Conscienza, forme, processi,*

ed. R. Battocchio and S. Noceti (Milan: Glossa, 2007), 163–79; P. Granfield, ed., *The Church and Communication* (Kansas City: Sheed & Ward, 1994); H.J. Pottmeyer, "Dialogue as a Model for Communication in the Church," in Granfield, ed., *Church as Communication*.

64. G. Ziviani, *Una chiesa di popolo. La parrocchia nel Vaticano II* (Bologna: EDB, 2011).

65. See F. Coccopalmerio, *La parrocchia tra Concilio Vaticano II e Codice di Diritto Canonico* (Milan: San Paolo, 2000); Paul VI, *Evangelii Nuntiandi* 58; Italian Bishops' Conference, *Evangelizzazione e sacramenti*, 94; *Comunione e comunità*, 42–44; *Comunicare il vangelo in un mondo che cambia*, 47, 50, 56–57; *The Missionary Face of the Parish* (2004); Congregation for the Clergy, Instruction, "The Pastoral Conversion of the Parish Community at the Service of the Church's Evangelizing Mission," www.vatican.va; Code of Canon Law (1983), cc. 515–72; CELAM, *Medellín Document, XV, Pastoral de conjuncto* 13–16; *Puebla Document* 105, 110–11, 617, 644, 650; *Notes Document* 170–77.

66. John Paul II, *Christifideles Laici* 26; see also 25–27, 61. *Catechesi Tradendae*, 67.

67. S. Dianich, "La teologia della parrocchia," in various authors, *Parrocchia e pastorale parrocchiale. Storia teologia e linee pastorali* (Bologna: EDB, 1986), 57–103, at 83.

68. F. Coccopalmerio, "La 'consultivit à' del consiglio pastorale parrocchiale e del Consiglio per gli affari economici della parrocchia," *Quaderni di Diritto Ecclesiale* 1 (1988): 60–65; A. Borras, "Petite apologie du conseil pastoral de paroisse," in *Communion ecclesiale et synodalité*, 23–80.

69. J. Avrile, "A propos du '*proprius sacerdos*': quelques réflexions sur les pouvoirs du prêtre de paroisse," in *Proceedings of the Fifth International Congress of Medieval Canon Law, Salamanca 21–25 September 1976*, ed. S. Kutter and K. Penningen (Vatican City: Biblioteca Apostolica Vaticana, 1980), 471–86; M. Medina Balam, "La función de enseñar del párroco," *Revista Mexicana de Derecho Canonico* 9, no. 2 (2003): 63–91; M. Rivella, "Il parroco come evangelizzatore," *Quaderni di Diritto Ecclesiale* 6 (1993): 22–28; G.P. Montini, "Il parroco *pastor proprius*: Il

significato di una formula," in *La parrocchia come chiesa locale*, Quaderni del seminario di Brescia 3 (Brescia: Morcelliana, 1993), 181–98.

70. The only exception is the Council for Economic Affairs, which must be involved in decisions. See M. Calvi, "Il Consiglio pastorale per gli affari economici," *Quaderni di Diritto Ecclesiale* 1 (1988): 20–33; D. Mogavero, "Il parroco e i sacerdoti suoi collaboratori," in *La parrocchia e i sacerdoti suoi collaboratori*, ed. A. Longhitano, F. Coccopalmerio, and G. Bonicelli (Bologna: EDB, 1987), 119–46.

71. See R. Collins, "Small Groups: An Experience of Church," *Louvain Studies* 13 (1988): 109–36.

72. J.G. Healey and J. Hinton, eds., *Small Christian Communities Today; Capturing the New Moment* (Nairobi: Pauline Publications Africa, 2006); A. Mringi, "Ecclesiology, Structures and Activities within SCCs," *The Jurist* 56 (1996): 200–240; T. Kleissler, M. Lebert, and J. Mcguiness, *Small Christian Communities: A Vision of Hope for the 21st Century* (New York / Mahwah, NJ: Paulist Press, 1997).

73. See A. Barreiro, *Basic Ecclesial Communities; The Evangelization of the Poor*, trans. Barbara Campbell (Maryknoll, NY: Orbis Books 1982); M. de Azevedo, *Basic Ecclesial Communities in Brazil: The Challenge of a New Way of Being Church* (Washington, DC: Georgetown University Press, 1987); C. Boff, "The Nature of Basic Christian Communities," *Concilium* 144 (1981): 53–58; R. Oliveros, "Iglesia Particular, Parroquia y CEBs," in *Aparecida: Renacer de una esperanza* (Dragoon, AZ: Fundacion Amerindia, 2007), 202–13.

74. CELAM, *Medellín Document* VI, III, 13.

75. CELAM, *Santo Domingo Document* 225.

76. CELAM, *Aparecida Document* 178.

77. CELAM, *Puebla Document* 96. See also 617.

78. CELAM, *Aparecida Document* 178. See also 179–80.

79. CELAM, *Aparecida Document* 172.

80. CELAM, *Aparecida Document* 178.

81. See CELAM, *Puebla Document* 644.

82. See A. Borras, "Délibérer en Eglise: communion ecclésiale et fidélité évangélique," *Nouvelle Revue Theologique* 132 (2010): 177–96;

Notes

P. Gherri, *Discerning and Choosing in the Church* (Rome: Lateran University Press, 2016).

83. N. Luhmann, *Organisation and Decision* (Milan: Bruno Mondadori, 2005), 101.

84. See chapter 2 of this book on the *sensus fidei/fidelium*.

85. See A. Borras, "Ecclesial Synodality, Participatory Processes and Decision-Making. Il punto di vista di un canonista," in *La riforma e le riforme nella chiesa*, ed., A. Spadaro and C.M. Galli (Brescia: Queriniana, 2016), 207–32.

86. See S. Noceti, "Elaborating Decisions in the Church. An Ecclesiological Reflection," in *Sinodalità. Dimension of the Church, Practices in the Church*, ed. R. Battocchio and L. Tonello (Padua: EMP, 2020), 237–54.

87. See J.G. March, *Decisions and Organisations* (Bologna: Il Mulino, 1993). See also G. Klein, *Sources of Power: How People Make Decisions* (Cambridge, MA: MIT Press, 1998); R. Rumiati, *Decidere. How to Choose the Best Path* (Bologna: Il Mulino, 2018).

88. Luhmann, *Organisation and Decision*, 50.

89. Y.M. Congar, "'Quod omnes tangit, ab omnibus tractari et approbari debet,'" *Revue historique de droit français et étranger* 36 (1958): 210–59. See ITC, "Synodality" 65.

90. J. Adair, *Decision Making and Problem Solving*, 2nd ed. (Milan: FrancoAngeli, 2018); see also D. Falcone, F. De Felice, and T.L. Saaty, *Il decision making e i sistemi decisionai multicriterio* (Milan: Hoepli, 2009); T.L. Saaty, *Decision Making for Leaders. The Analytic Hierarchy Process for Decision in a Complex World* (Pittsburgh, PA: RWS, 2012).

91. ITC, "Synodality," 74.

92. See A. Borras, "Votum tantum consultivum. Les limites ecclésiologiques d'une formule canonique," *Didaskalia* 45 (2015): 145–62; F. Coccopalmerio, "La 'consultività' del consiglio pastorale parrocchiale e del Consiglio per gli affari economici della parrocchia," *Quaderni di Diritto Ecclesiale* 1 (1988): 60–65.

93. See A. D'Auria, "Parere, consenso e responsabilità: il can 127," in GIDDC, *Il governo nel servizio della comunione ecclesiale* (Milan: Glossa, 2017), 59–100.

94. Cyprian of Carthage, *Epistle 14*.

95. See L. Angelini, et al., *Nuovi modelli di leadership partecipativa* (Milan: Guerini, 2021); M. Tushman and C. O'Reilly, *Winning through Innovation: A Practical Guide to Leading Organizational Change and Renewal* (Boston, MA: Harvard Business School Press, 1997); E.H. Schein, *Organizational culture and leadership* (Hoboken, NJ: Wiley, 2010); D. Campus, *Lo stile del leader. Deciding and Communicating in Contemporary Democracies* (Bologna: Il Mulino, 2016); V. De Giosa, *Leadership. Theory and Practice of Organisation* (Rome: Carocci, 2010).

96. See Code of Canon Law, c. 391 (the bishop is the only legislator for his diocese) and c. 466 (he is the only one who gives the decrees the form of law).

97. See G. Arbuckle, *Refounding the Church. Dissent for Leadership* (Maryknoll, NY: Orbis Books, 1993).

98. M. Mulder, *Toward Equalization through Participation* (1971), cited in A. Bryman, *Leadership and Organization* (London/ New York: Routledge, 1986/87).

99. G. Alberigo, "Ecclesiology and Democracy. Convergences and Divergences," *Concilium* 28 (1992): 737.

100. See L. Badini Confalonieri, *Democracy in the Christian Church* (London: T&T Clark, 2012); E. Bianchi and R. Radford Reuther, eds., *A Democratic Catholic Church: The Reconstruction of the Roman Catholic Church* (New York: Crossroad, 1993).

101. See G. Lafont, *La chiesa e il travaglio delle riforme* (Cinisello Balsamo: San Paolo, 2012), 251–52.

102. See B. Schimmelpfennig, "The Principle of the 'Sanior Pars' in the Choice of Bishops in the Middle Ages," *Concilium* 16, no. 7 (1980): 42–54.

103. ITC, "Synodality," 118–19.

Notes

CHAPTER 6

1. Francis, "Address Commemorating the Fiftieth Anniversary of the Institution of the Synod of Bishops," October 17, 2015, www.vatican.va.

2. See R. Luciani, *Synodality* (Mahwah, NJ: Paulist Press, 2022).

3. See H.M. Legrand, "Collégialité des évêques et communion des églises dans la réception de Vatican II," *Revue des Sciences Philosophiques et Théologiques* 75 (1991): 545–68; G. Alberigo, "La sinodalità dopo il Vaticano II," in *Vescovi per la speranza del mondo*, ed. M. Fabri dos Anjos (Bologna: EDB, 2001), 99–113.

4. Therefore, synodality must be the church's habitual and concrete *modus vivendi et operandi*.

5. H.M. Legrand, "Inverser Babel, mission de l'église," *Spiritus* 11 (1970): 323–46, at 334. See also Legrand, "The Development of Church-Subjects: An Instance of Vatican II. Theological Foundations and Institutional Reflections," *Christianity in History* 2 (1981): 129–64.

6. B. Lonergan, *Method in Theology* (New York: Herder and Herder, 1972), 379–85.

7. John Chrysostom, *Ex. in Psalm.* 149,2: *PG* 55,493. See R. della Rocca, "La sinodalità nella riflessione dei padri della chiesa," in *La sinodalità al tempo di papa Francesco, vol. 1*, ed. N. Salato (Bologna: EDB, 2020), 85–104.

8. G. Ruggieri, "I sinodi tra storia e teologia," in *Chiesa e sinodalità*, ed. R. Battocchio and S. Noceti, 129–61, at 160.

Selected Bibliography

CHURCH DOCUMENTS

Acta Synodalia Sacrosancti Concilii Oecumenici Vaticani II, 32 vols. Vatican City: Typis Polyglottis Vaticanis, 1970–99.

Code of Canon Law: Latin-English Edition. Washington, DC: Canon Law Society of America, 1999.

International Theological Commission. "Synodality in the Life and Mission of the Church," March 2, 2018. http://www.vatican.va.

Pope Francis. Address during the Apostolic Journey to Rio de Janeiro to the Leadership of the Episcopal Conferences of Latin America during the General Coordination Meeting. https://www.vatican.va.

———. Apostolic Exhortation *Evangelii Gaudium* (The Joy of the Gospel). November 24, 2013. https://w2.vatican.va.

———. Christmas Address to the Roman Curia. December 21, 2013. https://w2.vatican.va.

———. Christmas Address to the Roman Curia. December 22, 2014. https://w2.vatican.va.

———. Christmas Greetings to the Roman Curia. December 22, 2016. http://w2.vatican.va.

———. Christmas Address to the Roman Curia. December 21, 2020. http://www.vatican.va.

———. Discourse to the Curia. Christmas Greetings for the Roman Curia. December 22, 2014. http://www.vatican.va.

———. Letter to the People of God. August 20, 2018. http://www .vatican.va.

———. Morning Meditation, "L'acqua che scorre nella chiesa." November 9, 2013. https://w2.vatican.va.

———. Opening of the XV Ordinary General Assembly of the Synod of Bishops. Address at the opening of the Synod of Bishops on young people, the faith and vocational discernment. October 3, 2018. http://www.vatican.va.

———. Speech at the Commemoration of the 50th Anniversary of the Institution of the Synod of Bishops. October 17, 2015. http://w2.vatican.va.

Pope Paul VI. Address during the Last General Meeting of the Second Vatican Council. December 7, 1965. https://w2.vatican.va.

———. Apostolic Letter issued Motu proprio *Sollicitudo Omnium Ecclesiarum* (Care of All). June 24, 1969. http://www.vatican.va.

———. Apostolic Letter issued Motu proprio *Apostolica Sollicitudo* (Apostolic Concern). September 15, 1965. http://www.vatican.va.

———. Opening Speech at Vatican II Second Session. September 29, 1963. http://www.vatican.va.

———. Speech at the Beginning of Labors in the Synodal Hall. *Synodus Episcoporum*. September 30, 1967. https://w2.vatican.va.

Schemata Constitutionum et Decretorum de quibus disceptabitur in Concilii sessionibus: De Ecclesia et de B. Maria Virgine, Part II. Vatican City: Typis Polyglottis Vaticanis, 1962.

Second Vatican Council. Dogmatic Constitution on the Church *Lumen Gentium* (Light of the Nations). December 7, 1965. Holy See. http://www.vatican.va.

BOOKS

Aymans, Winfried. *Diritto canonico e comunione ecclesiale. Saggi di diritto canonico in prospecttiva theologica*. Turin: Giappichelli Editore, 1993.

Battocchio, Riccardo, and Livio Tonello, eds. *Sinodalità: Dimensione della Chiesa, pratiche nella Chiesa*. Padua: EMP, 2020.

————— and Serena Noceti. *Chiesa e sinodalità*. Milan: Glossa, 2007.

Bergoglio, Jorge Mario. *Letters of Tribulation*. Edited by Antonio Spadaro, SJ, and Diego Fares. Maryknoll, NY: Orbis Books, 2019.

CELAM. *Renovación y reestructuración del CELAM: Documento de Trabajo*. Bogotá: Celam Press, 2021.

Chapman, Mark D., and Vladimir Latinovic, eds. *Changing the Church: Transformations of Christian Belief, Practice, and Life*. Switzerland: Palgrave Macmillan, 2020.

Compte, María Teresa, and Rafael Luciani, eds. *En camino hacia una Iglesia Sinodal: de Pablo VI a Francisco*. Madrid: PPC, 2020.

Congar, Yves. *Por una Iglesia servidora y pobre*. Salamanca: San Esteban, 2014.

—————. *True and False Reform in the Church*. Collegeville, MN: Liturgical Press, 1950/2011.

Conway, Eamonn, Eugene Duffy, and Mary McDaid, eds. *The Synodal Pathway: When Rhetoric Meets Reality*. Dublin: Columba Press, 2022.

De Smedt, Emile-Joseph. *The Priesthood of the Faithful*. New York: Paulist Press, 1962.

Dianich, Severino. *Diritto e teologia. Ecclesiologia e canonistica per una riforma della Chiesa*. Bologna: EDB, 2015.

—————. *Riforma della Chiesa e ordinamento canónico*. Bologna: EDB, 2018.

————— and Serena Noceti. *Trattato sulla Chiesa*. Brescia: Queriniana, 2002.

Duch, Lluís. *Educación y crisis de la modernidad*. Barcelona: Paidós, 1997.

Dulles, Avery. *Church and Society: The Laurence J. McGinley Lectures, 1988–2007*. New York: Fordham University Press, 2008.

Faggioli, Massimo, and Andrea Vicini, eds. *The Legacy of Vatican II*. Mahwah, NJ: Paulist Press 2015.

Fegert, Jörg, Michael Kölch, Elisa König, et al., eds. *Schutz vor sexueller Gewalt und Übergriffen in Institutionen*. Ulm: Springer, Universitätsklinikum, 2018.

Finucane, Daniel J. *Sensus Fidelium: The Use of a Concept in the Post–Vatican II Era.* Eugene, OR: Wipf & Stock, 1996/2016.

Galli, Carlos M., and Antonio Spadaro, SJ, eds. *For a Missionary Reform of the Church: The Civiltà Cattolica Seminar.* Mahwah, NJ: Paulist Press, 2017.

—————. *La riforma e le riforme nella Chiesa.* Brescia: Queriniana, 2016.

Hünermann, Peter, and Bernd Jochen Hilberath, eds. *Herders Theologischer Kommentar zum Zweiten Vatikanischen Konzil,* vol. 2. Freiburg: Herder, 2004.

Luciani, Rafael, and María del Pilar Silveira, eds. *La sinodalidad en la vida de la Iglesia: Reflexiones para contribuir a la reforma eclesial.* Madrid: San Pablo, 2020.

—————. *Pope Francis and the Theology of the People.* Maryknoll: NY: Orbis Books, 2017.

—————, and Carlos Schickendantz, eds. *Reforma de estructuras y conversión de mentalidades. Retos y desafíos para una Iglesia Sinodal.* Madrid: KHAF, 2020.

—————, Serena Noceti, and Carlos Schickendantz, eds. *Sinodalità e riforma: una sfida ecclesiale.* Brescia: Queriniana, 2022. Translated from the Spanish: *Sinodalidad y reforma. Un desafío eclesial.* Madrid: PPC, 2022.

Madrigal Terrazas, Jesús Santiago. *Unas lecciones sobre el Vaticano II y su legado.* Madrid: San Pablo, 2012.

Muñoz, Ronaldo. *Nueva conciencia de la Iglesia en América Latina.* Salamanca: Sígueme, 1974.

Noceti, Serena, and Roberto Repole, eds. *Commentario ai documenti del Vaticano II,* vol. 2. Bologna: EDB, 2015.

Philips, Gérard. *La Iglesia y su misterio en el Concilio Vaticano II: Historia y comentario de la Constitución Lumen Gentium,* vol. 1. Barcelona: Herder, 1968.

Pié-Ninot, Salvador. *La sacramentalidad de la comunidad cristiana.* Salamanca: Cristiandad, 2007.

Selected Bibliography

Portillo, Daniel, ed. *Tolerancia Cero*. México-Madrid: CEPROME-PPC, 2019.

Rahner, Karl. *The Shape of the Church to Come*. London: SPCK, 1974.

―――. *Strukturwandel der Kirche als Aufgabe und Chance*. Freiburg-Basel-Vienna: Herder, 1972.

―――― and Joseph Ratzinger. *Episcopado y primado*. Barcelona: Herder, 1961/2005.

Rivella, Mauro. *Partecipazione e corresponsabilità nella Chiesa*. Milano: Ancora, 2000.

Scannone, J. C., et al. *Iglesia universal. Iglesias particulares*. Buenos Aires: San Pablo, 2000.

Suenens, León Joseph. *Coresponsibility in the Church*. New York: Herder and Herder, 1968.

Trigo, Pedro. *Concilio Plenario Venezolano: Una constituyente para nuestras Iglesia*. Caracas: Centro Gumilla, 2009.

Vitali, Dario. *Lumen Gentium: Storia, commento, recezione*. Rome: Studium, 2012.

ARTICLES

Arrieta, Juan Ignacio. "Órganos de participación y corresponsabilidad en la Iglesia diocesana." *Ius Canonicum* 34, no. 68 (1994).

Bayona Aznar, Bernardo. "Nacimiento, letargo y renacimiento de la colegialidad en el Concilio Vaticano II." *Didaskalia* 45, no. 1 (2015): 117–34.

Beal, John P. "Consultation in Church Governance: Taking Care of Business by Taking after Business." *Canon Law Society of America. Proceedings* 68 (2006): 25–54.

Becquart, XMCJ, Nathalie. "The Synod on Young People, a Laboratory of Synodality." *International Bulletin of Mission Research* (2020). https://journals.sagepub.com/doi/full/10.1177/2396 939320951566.

Borras, Alphonse. "Trois expressions de la synodalité depuis Vatican II." *Ephemerides Theologicae Lovanienses* 90, no. 4 (2014).

———. *"Votum tantum consultivum.* Les limites ecclesiologiques d'une formule canonique." *Didaskalia* 45, no. 1 (2015).

Congar, Yves. "The Church: The People of God." *Concilium* 1, no. 1 (1965): 7–36.

———. "Quod omnes tangit ab omnibus tractari et opprobari debet." *Revue historique de droit français et étranger* 36 (1958): 210–59.

———. "Renovación del espíritu y reforma de la institución." *Concilium* 73 (1972): 326–37.

Fernández, Víctor Manuel. "El sensus populi: la legitimidad de una teología desde el pueblo." *Teología* 72 (1998).

Fornés, Juan. "Notas sobre el 'Duo sunt genera Christianorum' del Decreto de Graciano." *Ius Canonicum* 30, no. 60 (1990): 607–32.

Franck, Bernard. "Les expériences synodales après Vatican II." *Communio* 3, no. 3 (1978).

Gera, Lucio. "Puebla: evangelización de la cultura." *Teología* 16, no. 33 (1979).

Interview with Cardinal Léon-Joseph Suenens, "La unidad de la Iglesia en la lógica del Vaticano II: El cardenal Suenens contesta las preguntas de José Broucker," *El Ciervo* 18, no. 184 (1969). https://www.jstor.org/stable/40803679.

Legrand, Hervé. "L'articolazione tra le Chiese locali, Chiese regionali e Chiesa universale." *Ad Gentes: Teologia e Antropologia della Missione* 3, no. 1 (1999).

———. "Lo sviluppo di chiese-soggetto: un'istanza del Vaticano II." *Cristianesimo nella Storia* 2, no. 1 (1981).

Luciani, Rafael. "Lo que afecta a todos debe ser tratado y aprobado por todos: Hacia estructuras de participación y poder de decisión compartido." *Revista CLAR* 53, no. 1 (2020): 59–66.

———. "Medellín como acontecimiento sinodal: Una eclesialidad colegiada fecundada y completada." *Revista Horizontes* 50 (2018): 482–516.

————. "Medellín Fifty Years Later: From Development to Liberation." *Theological Studies* 79, no. 3 (2018): 566–89.

Parra, SJ, Alberto. "El proceso de sacerdotalización, Una histórica interpretación de los ministerios eclesiales." *Theologica Xaveriana* 28, no. 1 (1978).

Pope Francis. Interview with Antonio Spadaro, SJ. "Clericalism—that desire to lord it over lay people—signifies an erroneous and destructive separation of the clergy, a type of narcissism." *L'Osservatore Romano* 45, no. 39, September 27, 2013.

————. "The Sovereignty of the People of God. Meeting of the Pope with the Jesuits of Mozambique and Madagascar." *La Civiltà Cattolica*, September 5, 2019. https://www.laciviltacattolica.com.

Roncagliolo, Cristián. "Iglesia en salida: una aproximación teológico pastoral al concepto de Iglesia en Evangelii Gaudium." *Teología y Vida* 55, no. 2 (2014).

Routhier, Gilles. "Évangilie et modèle de sociabilité." *Laval Théologique et Philosophique* 51, no. 1 (1995).

————. "La synodalitè dans l'église locale." *Scripta Theologica* 48, no. 3 (2016).

Schickendantz, Carlos. "Estudios sistemático-hermenéuticos sobre el Vaticano II: Tres aportes relevantes en el período posconciliar." *Veritas* 30 (2014): 187–211.

ONLINE RESOURCES

Royal Commission into Institutional Responses to Child Sexual Abuse, "Religious Institutions," in *Final Report*. Canberra: Commonwealth of Australia, 2017. https://www.childabuseroyalcommission.gov.au/final-report.

"Sexueller Missbrauch an Minderjährigen durch katholische Priester, Diakone und männliche Ordensangehörige im Bereich der Deutschen Bischofskonferenz." Mannheim-Heidelberg-Giessen, September

2018. https://bistumlimburg.de/fileadmin/redaktion/Bereiche/missbrauch/MHG-Studie-gesamt.pdf.

"The Causes and Context of Sexual Abuse of Minors by the Catholic Church in the United States between 1950–2010," 87.91.92. Study by John Jay College of Criminal Justice of City University of New York at the request of the U.S. Catholic Bishops' Conference, 2002. https://www.lib.latrobe.edu.au/research/ageofinquiry/biogs/E000235b.htm.

Pope Francis. Video message October 8, 2020. https://www.vaticannews.va/es/papa/news/2020-10/video-papa.html.

ADDITIONAL RESOURCES ON SYNODALITY

Books and Book Chapters

Aymans, Winfried. *Das synodale Element in der Kirchenverfassung.* Munich: Max Hueber Verlag, 1970.

Borras, Alphonse. *Communion ecclésiale et synodalité.* Paris: Éditions CLD, 2019.

Calabrese, Gianfranco. *Ecclesiologia sinodale.* Bologna: EDB, 2021.

Chapman, Mark D., and Vladimir Latinovic, eds. *Changing the Church: Transformations of Christian Belief, Practice, and Life.* Switzerland: Palgrave Macmillan, 2020.

Comblin, José. *People of God.* Maryknoll, NY: Orbis Books, 2004.

Compte, María Teresa, and Rafael Luciani, eds. *En camino hacia una Iglesia Sinodal: de Pablo VI a Francisco.* Madrid: PPC, 2020.

Congar, Yves. *De la communion des Églises à une ecclésiologie de l'Église universelle.* Paris: Editions du Cerf, 1962.

Gaillardetz, Richard R. *By What Authority? Foundations for Understanding Authority in the Church.* Collegeville, MN: Liturgical Press, 2018.

Graulich, Marcus, and Johanna Rahner, eds. *Synodalität in der Katolischen Kirche.* Freiburg: Herder, 2020.

Selected Bibliography

Hinze, Bradford E. "Synodality and Democracy: For We the People," in Christoph Böttigheimer, ed., *Vaticanum 21: Die bleibenden Aufgaben des Zweiten Vatikanischen Konzils im 21. Jahrhundert: Dokumentationsband zum Münchner Kongress "Das Konzil 'eröffnen.'"* Freiburg im Breisgau, Herder, 2016.

Hünermann, Peter. "Autorität und Synodalität. Eine Gründfrage der Ekklesiologie." In *Autorität und Synodalität. Eine interdisziplinäre und interkonfessionelle Umschau nach ökumenischen Chancen und ekklesiogischen Desideraten*, edited by C. Böttigheimer and J. Hoffman, 321–48. Frankfurt: O. Lembeck, 2008.

Kelly, Thomas, and Bob Pennington. *Bridge Building. Pope Francis' Practical Theological Approach*. New York: Crossroad, 2020.

Komonchak, Joseph A. "Theological Perspectives on the Exercise of Synodality." In *Il Sinodo dei Vescovi al servizio di una Chiesa sinodale*, edited by Lorenzo Baldisseri. Vatican City: Libreria Editrice Vaticana, 2016.

Luciani, Rafael. "La renovación en la jerarquía eclesial por sí misma no genera la transformación. Situar la colegialidad al interno de la sinodalidad." In *Teología y prevención: Estudio sobre los abusos sexuales en la Iglesia*, edited by Daniel Portillo, 37–64. Santander: Sal Terrae, 2020.

Mayer, Anne Marie C., ed. *The Letter and the Spirit: On the Forgotten Documents of Vatican II*. Leuven: Peeters, 2018.

Meloni, Alberto, and Silvia Scatena, eds. *Synod and Synodality: Theology, History, Canon Law and Ecumenism*. Münster: LIT Verlag, 2005.

Noceti, Serena. "Riforma e sinodalità: un interessante binomio." In *Sinodalità. Del popolo di Dio?*, edited by Cettina Militello, 22–52. Trapani: Il Pozzo di Giacobbe, 2022.

Pope, Stephen, ed. *Common Calling: The Laity and Governance of the Catholic Church*. Washington, DC: Georgetown University Press, 2004.

Repole, Roberto. *La Chiesa e il suo dono*. Brescia: Queriniana, 2019.

Routhier, Gilles, and Joseph Famerée. *Penser la réforme de l`Église*. Paris: Editions du Cerf, 2021.

Ruggieri, Giuseppe. *Chiesa sinodale*. Rome: Laterza, 2017.

Sartorio, Ugo. *Sinodalità*. Milan: Ancora 2021.

Szabó, Peter, ed. *Primacy and Synodality: Deepening Insights. Proceedings of the 23rd Congress of the Society for the Law of the Eastern Churches, Debrecen, September 3–8, 2017. Kanon XXV.* Nyíregyháza: St. Athanasius Greek-Catholic Theological Institute, 2019.

Tillard, Jean-Marie R. *Church of Churches. The Ecclesiology of Communion.* Collegeville, MN: Liturgical Press, 1992.

Articles

Antón, Angel. "Strutture sinodali dopo il Concilio. Sinodo dei vescovi, Conferenze Episcopali." *Credere Oggi* 13, no. 4 (1993): 85–105.

Arderí, Raúl. "Una experiencia sinodal en la Iglesia cubana." *Razón y Fe* 283, no. 1451 (2021): 303–13.

Azcuy, Virginia. "The Tensions in the Church Today: Four Fundamental Challenges." *Concilium* 4 (2018): 47–58.

Beal, John P. "The Exercise of the Power of Governance by Lay People: State of the Question." *Jurist* 55, no. 1 (1995): 1–92.

Borras, Alphonse. "La Conférence ecclésiale de l'Amazonie: une institution synodale inédite." *Ephemerides Theologicae Lovanienses* 97, no. 2 (2021): 223–92.

———. "Episcopalis Communio, mérites et limites d`une réforme institutionnelle." *Nouvelle Revue Théologique* 141 (2019): 66–88.

Clifford, Catherine E. "Emerging Consensus on Collegiality and Catholic Ecumenical Responsibility." *The Jurist* 64 (2004): 332–60.

Coda, Piero. "The Way of the Church in the Third Millenium." *Proche-Orient Chrétien* 68, nos. 3–4 (2018): 316–25.

Consuelo Vélez, Olga. "Teología feminista latinoamericana de la liberación." *Horizonte* 32 (2013): 1801–12.

Duffy, Eugene. "Processes for communal discernment: Diocesan synods and assemblies." *The Jurist* 71 (2011): 77–90.

Selected Bibliography

Galli, Carlos María. "Constitución de la Conferencia Eclesial de la Amazonía. Fundamentos históricos, teológicos, culturales y pastorales." *Revista Medellín* 179 (2020): 517–42.

Haers, Jacques. "A Synodal Process on Synodality: Synodal Missionary Journeying and Common Apostolic Discernment." *Louvain Studies* 43 (2020): 215–38.

Kasper, Walter. "Petrine Ministry and Synodality." *The Jurist* 66 (2006): 298–309.

Komonchak, Joseph, A. "The Local Church and the Church Catholic: The Contemporary Theological Problematic." *The Jurist* 52 (1992): 416–47.

———. "People of God, Hierarchical Structure, and Communion: An Easy Fit?" *Canon Law Society of America. Proceedings of the Sixteenth Annual Convention* 60 (1998): 91–102.

———. "The Status of the Faithful in the Revised Code of Canon Law." *Concilium* 147 (1981): 37–45.

———. "The Synod of 1985 and the Notion of the Church." *Chicago Studies* 26 (1987): 330–45.

Legrand, Hervé. "Reception, *Sensus Fidelium*, and Synodal Life: An Effort at Articulation." *The Jurist* 57 (1997): 405–31.

———. "La sinodalità, dimensione inerente allá vita ecclesiale: Fondamienti ed attualità." *Vivens Homo* 15 (2005): 5–42.

Luciani, Rafael. "The Centrality of the People in Pope Francis' Sociocultural Theology." *Concilium* 3 (2018): 55–68.

———. "Hacia una eclesialidad sinodal." *Revista Horizontes* 59 (2021).

———. "Medellín as Synodal Event: The Genesis and Development of a Collegial Ecclesiality." *Studia Canonica* 53, no. 1 (2019): 183–208.

———. "Reconfigurar la identidad y la estructura eclesial a la luz de las Iglesias locales. Querida Amazonia y el estatuto teológico de las realidades socioculturales." *Revista Medellín* 46, no. 179 (2020): 487–515.

Madrigal Terrazas, Jesús Santiago. "La conversión del papado en una Iglesia sinodal." *Medellín* 43, no. 168 (2017): 313–31.

———. "Sínodo es nombre de Iglesia. Corresponsabilidad, autoridad y participación." *Sal Terrae* 89, no. 1043 (2001): 197–212.

Mayer, Anne Marie C. "For a Synodal Church. Equipping the Catholic Church on Her Way into the Third Millennium." *Louvain Studies* 43 (2020): 205–14.

Noceti, Serena. "*Sensus fidelium* e dinamiche ecclesiali." *Marriage, Families and Spirituality* 23, no. 1 (2017): 86–98.

———. "What Structures Are Needed for a Reform of the Church?" *Concilium* 4 (2018): 85–91.

Ombres, Robert. "The Synod of Bishops: Canon Law and Ecclesial Dynamics." *Ecclesiastical Law Journal* 16, no. 3 (2014): 306–18.

Oshaim, Amanda. "Stepping toward a Synodal Church," *Theological Studies* 80 (2019): 370–92.

Pottmeyer, Hermann J. "The Plena et Suprema Potestatis Jurisdictionis of the Pope at the First Vatican Council and Receptio." *The Jurist* 57 (1997): 216–34.

Rahner, Karl, SJ. "Towards a Fundamental Theological Interpretation of Vatican II." *Theological Studies* 40, no. 4 (1979): 716–27.

Renken, John A. "Synodality: A Constitutive Element of the Church. Reflections on Pope Francis and Synodality." *Studia Canonica* 52, no. 1 (2018): 5–44.

Routhier, Gilles. "La synodalitè dans l'Église locale." *Scripta Theologica* 48 (2016): 687–706.

Rush, Ormond. "Inverting the Pyramid. The Sensus Fidelium in a Synodal Church." *Theological Studies* 78, no. 2 (2017): 299–325.

———. "*Sensus Fidei*: Faith Making Sense of Revelation." *Theological Studies* 62, no. 2 (2001): 231–61.

Scannone, Juan Carlos. "Pope Francis and the Theology of the People." *Theological Studies* 77 (2016): 118–35.

Schickendantz, Carlos. "Fracaso institucional de un modelo teológico-cultural de Iglesia. Factores sistémicos en la crisis de los abusos." *Teología y Vida* 60 (2019): 9–40.

———. "La reforma de la Iglesia en clave sinodal," *Teología y Vida* 58 (2017): 35–60.

Schmiedl, Joachim. "Es braucht einen neuen Dialog: Theologen und Bischöfe entdecken das Prinzip der Synodalität." *Herder Korrespondenz* 70, no. 4 (2016): 48–49.

———. "Synodalität. Eine Perspektive für die katholische Kirche." *Lebendige Seelsorge* 69, no. 4 (2018): 234–38.

Szabó, Péter. "Episcopal Conferences, Particular Councils, and the Renewal of Inter-Diocesan 'Deliberative Synodality.'" *Studia Canonica* 53, no. 1 (2019): 265–96.

Vitali, Dario. "Sensus fidelium e opinione pubblica nella Chiesa." *Gregorianum* 82 (2001): 689–717.

Wijlens, Myriam. "Exercising Collegiality in a Supra-National or Continental Institution such as the FABC, CCEE, and ComECE." *The Jurist* 64 (2004):168–204.

———. "Reforming the Church by Hitting the Reset Button: Reconfiguring Collegiality within Synodality because of Sensus Fidei Fidelium." *The Canonist* 8 (2017): 235–61.

———. "Representation and Witnessing in Synodal Structures. Rethinking the Munus Docendi of Episcopal Conferences in Light of Communio Fidelium, Communio Ecclesiarum and Communio Episcoparum." *Studia Canonica* 53 (2019): 75–105.